Kingston Libraries

This item can be returned or renewed at a Kingston Borough Library on or before the latest date stamped below. If the item is not reserved by another reader it may be renewed by telephone up to a maximum of three times by quoting your membership number. Only items issued for the standard three-week loan period are renewable.

www.kingston.gov.uk/libraries

THE THUNDER MUTTERS

also by Alice Oswald

The Thunder Mutters

101 Poems for the Planet

EDITED BY ALICE OSWALD

faber and faber

First published in 2005
by Faber and Faber Limited
3 Queen Square London WC1N 3AU

Photoset by Refine Catch Ltd, Bungay, Suffolk
Printed in England by Mackays of Chatham plc, Chatham, Kent

The illustration on page 169 is reproduced
by permission of the artist, Kathleen Lindsley

A CIP record for this book
is available from the British Library

ISBN 0−571−21854−7

10 9 8 7 6 5 4 3 2 1

Contents

Introduction: A Dew's Harp ix

CONTENTS [vi

Introduction: A Dew's Harp

A dew's harp is a rake (in old Devon dialect). This book is dedicated to the rake, which I see as a rhythmical but not predictable instrument that connects the earth to our hands. Raking, like any outdoor work, is a more mobile, more many-sided way of knowing a place than looking. When you rake leaves for a couple of hours, you can hear right into the non-human world, it's as if you and the trees had found a meeting point in the sound of the rake. Murray Schafer, one of a growing number of acoustic ecologists, divides music into two tribes: that of the flute, which represents 'internal music breaking forth from the human breast', and that of the lyre, which is 'external sound, god-sent'. While the flautist sighs out his sounds, the lyre player's task is to discover 'the sonic properties already there in the materials of the universe', which is as good a description as any of what this book's about. Those who play the dew's harp are, as it were, running their fingers over the leaves, listening in, finding what's already there.

All the following poems lie somewhere along this line of encounter between a human and his context. At one end, there are those work poems in which 'work begins to yield a language that puts you and something else at a point of vibrant intersection' (Poirier): songs for lowering anchors or for cutting cotton, poems by Clare, Frost, Kavanagh. At the other end there are poems in which the human has crossed over, and disintegrated in the non-human: metamorphosis poems like 'John Barleycorn' and the 'Song of the Murdered Child', as well as found or chance-constrained poems like Marinetti's 'A Landscape Heard', Drayton's topographical epic, Lawrence's 'poetry of that which is at hand'. Between these two extremes, there are any number of portraits of the half-human, half-animal state in which most of us spend our lives. What qualifies these for inclusion is sometimes little more than a hunch that the transfiguring process has begun – the feeling of nature pulling a man back into the ground that runs through such diverse poems as Heaney's 'Bog Queen', Burnside's 'Heat Wave', Beckett's 'From an Abandoned Work', or the anonymous epitaph to Henry Clarke who slept in hayricks and paced himself to the rhythms of tides and birdsong.

No prospects, pastorals or nostalgic poems are in here, no poem that mistakes the matter at the end of the rake for a mere conceit. The knack of enervating nature (which starts in literature and quickly spreads to everything we touch) is an obstacle to ecology which can only be countered by a kind of porousness or sorcery that brings living things unmediated into the text. For that reason, I've favoured restless poems, poems that keep filling up with fresh looks; in particular those that follow the structure of oral poetry, which tends to be accretive rather than syntactic:– for example, Whitman's 'Leaves of Grass' or Ashbery's 'Into the Dusk-charged Air', as well as plenty of true oral poems. At their best they work like lists, little heaps of self-sufficient sentences that keep the poem open to the many-centred energies of the natural world.

Each poem has been placed between similar or related poems, so the anthology, though it has no themed divisions, has at least an emergent, overlapping structure. The poems come in drifts. They don't pronounce any one ecological message. Their work is to tinker with our locks, thereby putting our inner worlds in contact with the outer world – a deep, slow process that used to be the remit of the rake. In the seven or so years since I stopped full-time gardening, the petrol-driven leaf-blower, which requires its user to wear earphones, helmet and visor, has almost entirely replaced the rake in most large gardens. This book has nothing to do with the leaf-blower.

The Thunder Mutters

'The thunder mutters louder and more loud'

The thunder mutters louder and more loud
With quicker motion hay folks ply the rake
Ready to burst slow sails the pitch black cloud
And all the gang a bigger haycock make
To sit beneath – the woodland winds awake
The drops so large wet all thro' in an hour
A tiney flood runs down the leaning rake
In the sweet hay yet dry the hay folks cower
And some beneath the waggon shun the shower

We Field-Women

How it rained
When we worked at Flintcomb-Ash,
And could not stand upon the hill
Trimming swedes for the slicing-mill.
The wet washed through us – plash, plash, plash:
How it rained!

How it snowed
When we crossed from Flintcomb-Ash
To the Great Barn for drawing reed,
Since we could nowise chop a swede. –
Flakes in each doorway and casement-sash:
How it snowed!

How it shone
When we went from Flintcomb-Ash
To start at dairywork once more
In the laughing meads, with cows three-score,
And pails, and songs, and love – too rash:
How it shone!

Rains

Rain which in your most regrettable overflowings never forgets
the way the girls of Chiriqui suddenly pull out from between
    their darkened breasts lamps made out of flickering
    glow-worms
Rain capable of absolutely anything except washing away the
    bloodstains on the fingertips of assassins of entire peoples
    startled beneath the tall treetops of innocence

Translated from the French
by Michael Benedikt

Song

[*from* Twelfth Night]

When that I was and a little tiny boy,
  with hey, ho, the winde and the raine:
A foolish thing was but a toy,
  for the raine it raineth every day.

But when I came to mans estate,
  with hey ho, the winde and the raine:
Gainst Knaves and Theeves men shut their gate,
  for the raine it raineth every day.

But when I came alas to wive,
  with hey ho, the winde and the raine:
By swaggering could I never thrive,
  for the raine it raineth every day.

But when I came unto my beds,
  with hey ho, the winde and the raine:
With tosspottes still had drunken heades,
  for the raine it raineth every day.

A great while ago the world begon,
  hey ho, the winde and the raine:
But that's all one, our play is done,
  and wee'l strive to please you every day.

Epitaph at Bideford

Sacred to the memory of Captain Henry Clark
of this town
who departed this life 28th April 1836
aged 61 years

Our worthy FRIEND who lies beneath this stone
Was master of a vessel all his own
Houses and land had he and gold in store.
He spent the whole and would if ten times more.

For thirty years he scarce slept in a BED.
Linhays and limekilns lulled his weary head.
Because he would not to the Poorhouse go.
For his proud spirit would not let him to.

The blackbirds whistling notes at break of day
Used to awake him from his BED of HAY.
Unto the Bridge and quay he then repaired
To see what shipping up the River steered.

Oft in the week he used to view the Bay
To see what ships were coming in from sea.
To captains' wives he brought the welcome news
And to the relatives of all their crews.

At last poor Harry Clark was taken ill
And carried to the workhouse gainst his will
But being of this mortal life quite tired
He lived about a month and then expired.

ANONYMOUS

Mister Stormalong

1 Old Stormy he is dead an' gorn,
　　Chorus: To me way you Stormalong!
　Old Stormy he is dead an' gorn,
　　Chorus: Ay! ay! ay! Mister Stormalong!

2 Of all ol' skippers he was best,
　　But now he's dead an' gone to rest,

3 He slipped his cable off Cape Horn,
　　Close by the place where he was born.

4 Oh, off Cape Horn where he was born,
　　Our sails wuz torn an' our mainmast gorn.

5 We'll dig his grave with a silver spade.
　　His shroud of finest silk was made.

6 We lowered him down with a golden chain,
　　Our eyes all dim with more than rain.

7 He lies low in his salt-sea bed,
　　Our hearts are sore, our eyes wuz red.

8 An able seaman bold an' true,
　　A good ol' skipper to his crew.

9 He's moored at last an' furled his sail,
　　No danger now from wreck or gale.

10 Old Stormy heard the Angel call,
　　So sing his dirge now one an' all.

11 Oh, now we'll sing his funeral song,
　　Oh, roll her over, long an' strong.

ANONYMOUS   [8

12 Old Stormy loved a sailors' song,
      His voice wuz tough an' rough an' strong.

13 His heart wuz good an' kind an' soft,
      But now he's gone 'way up aloft.

14 For fifty years he sailed the seas,
      In winter gale and summer breeze.

15 But now Ol' Stormy's day is done;
      We marked the spot where he is gone.

16 So we sunk him under with a long, long roll,
      Where the sharks'll have his body, an' the divil have his soul.

17 An' so Ol' Stormy's day wuz done,
      South fifty six, west fifty one.

18 Ol' Stormy wuz a seaman bold,
      A Grand Ol' Man o' the days of old.

The Wreck of the *Swan*

Even so – as a man at the end tries no more
To escape but deliberately turns and plunges
Into the press of his foes and perishes there –
I remember the lesson of the wreck of the *Swan*,
Within her own home harbour and under the lights
Of her crew's native city, swept to doom on Christmas Eve.

The lights were warm on happy family parties
In hundreds of homes. – One wonders
If a man or woman here and there did not part
The curtains to look out and think how black
Was the night, and foul for men at sea.

Few could know that quite near at hand, just beyond
The bald fisher-rows of Footdee, the crew
In the lifeboat *Emma Constance* were fighting to save
Five men in the wheelhouse of that trawler, the *Swan*,
That wallowed in broken seas.

It was not what a seaman would call rough in the channel
But there was a heavy run of broken water
Along the inside wall of the North Pier
And for some reason unknown the *Swan* grounded
Two hundred yards within the pier-head,
Swung round, held fast, and took to labouring
In a welter of breakers and spray.

Less than ten minutes later a gun
Fired a rocket from the Pier and a line
For the breeches-buoy was across the *Swan*.
Had it been accepted that would have ended the tale.
But the men of the *Swan* – who knows why? –
Refused that line of safety.

HUGH MACDIARMID   [10

Meanwhile, with the celerity of firemen, the lifeboat crew,
Had assembled and tumbled into their powerful sixty-foot boat,
And she was off, and, in a few minutes, alongside the *Swan*,
Between that helpless ship and the pier.
Again the door of safety was wide open to the men of the *Swan*
And again they refused to pass through it.

The coxswain of the lifeboat roared at them,
Through his megaphone, to jump; but the five men
Of the *Swan* turned away and took refuge
In their doomed ship's wheelhouse instead.
There is a dark fascination in trying to appreciate
The spiritual inwardness of that strange situation.
Five men, for their own good reasons, refusing
To leave the shelter of their wheelhouse, while the lifeboat laboured
In the seas and the darkness, its crew dedicated to rescue,
Shouting to them in vain to come out and be saved.

A great wave hissing angrily came down on the lifeboat
And broke her adrift from the wreck.
Wielding the force of many tons it threw her
Against the foundations of the pier.
Along the length of 100 feet of solid masonry
She was flung like a piece of stick.

But the coxswain got her out again – a feat of seamanship
To hold the imagination in itself! –
And back alongside the *Swan* the *Emma Constance* went,
And again the lines were thrown,
But none of the men in the wheelhouse
Would come out to make them fast.

This time they had refused their last chance,
A sea of enormous weight broke over the wreck.
It carried away the upper part of the wheelhouse.

It swept the *Emma Constance* once more
Against the adamant wall of the pier.

This is the story of the men who wouldn't come out.
They were never seen alive again – and the coxswain and crew of
    the lifeboat
Carry the dark knowledge that up against
Something more formidable, more mysterious even,
Than wind and wave they battled largely in vain.

Four times they had gone back to that tragic wreck,
Manoeuvred with high skill in the cauldron 'twixt ship and pier,
Played the searchlight continuously on the battered bridge,
Cruised about for an hour,
But the men of the *Swan* refused to come out!

No dreamers these but hard-bitten men
Used to all the tortures of Old Feathery Legs
– The black villain who rides every crested wave
North of 65 degrees – he and his accursed legions,
The fog, the blizzard, the black-squall and the hurricane.

Up to their waists in water on the foredeck,
Gutting fish in the pounds, a black-squall
Screaming around, and the temperature 40 degrees below,
Working like automatons, 30 . . . 40 . . . 50 hours,
Grafting like fiends, with never a break or blink of sleep between.

A wave as high as the mast-heads crashing on deck
And sweeping all hands in a heap on the lee-scuppers,
Their arms and hands clawing up through the boiling surf
Still grasping wriggling fish and gutting knives.

And every now and then a message like this
Throbbing out of the black box.

'VALKYRIE calling all trawlers! . . . He's got us . . . Old Feathery's got us at last . . . We can see the rocks now . . . just astern . . . Another minute, I reckon! . . . We're on! . . . Good-bye, pals . . . Say good-bye to my wife . . . to my kiddies! . . . Good-bye, Buckie . . . Good-bye, Scotland!'

In 31 years at sea, he'd spent less
Than four years ashore, mostly in spells
On an average of 36 hours
Between trips – that's the price
His wife and kids had to pay for fish.

Time the public knew what these men have to face.

Nearly 100,000 of them at sea.
Nor are they the only men concerned.
Shipbuilders, rope, net and box manufacturers,
Fish-friers, buyers, retailers, salesmen,
Railways and road transport,
Coal, salt, and ice industries,
– About 3,000,000 folk would have to look elsewhere
For their bread and butter
If there were no trawlermen – or fish.

'Stand by all hands!' Down below
The lads along the starboard scuppers,
Backs bent, hands clawing the net,
Long as the ship, wide as a street,
Keyed to high-tension point,
Every muscle tense and taut.
'Shooto!' Over she goes.

Off the South-East coast of Iceland,
The East Horns, a famous landmark,
About five miles off the port-quarter.

All along the coast the great, barren, sullen mountains,
Eternally snow-crested, and shaped
Like monstrous crouching animals,
Sweep down to the water line,
And many a brave ship lies
Under the lowering evil shadows
Of the terrible rocks.

The successful skippers read the 'fish sign'
In a thousand different ways.
The gulls, the wind, currents, tides,
The depth of water, the nature of the bottom,
The type of fish caught in certain patches,
The nature of the food in their stomachs
Exposed by the gutting knife,
These factors and a thousand others
Supply information to be had or read
Only after years of battle and bitter experience.

Trawling along the lip of a marine mountain,
Covered by 200 fathoms of water,
On what is veritably a narrow mountain pass,
Scooping up hard 'sprags' (cod)
And 'ducks' (haddocks),
Each net sweeping up fish in hundreds of thousands,
Towing for miles over an area wide as a town.

The skipper has been on the bridge
For nearly 60 hours on end,
Down below, in the fish-pounds for'ard,
The lads are reeling like drunken men,
The decks awash, swirling high
As their arm-pits, and icy-cold.

These men are no dreamers.

Rex est qui metuit nihil.

A true man chooses death as he can in no part lie to a girl
But will put himself conscientiously into the worst possible light.

Töten ist eine Gestalt unseres wandernden Trauerns . . .
Rein ist im heiteren Geist,
Was an uns selber geschieht.[1]

(Killing is only a form of the sorrow we wander in here . . .
The serener spirit finds pure
All that can happen to us.)

'Death is ugly.
Tomato is crashing to.'[2]

The Gaels never die! They either 'change' or 'travel'.

'Happy the folk upon whom the Bear looks down, happy in this
error, whom of fears the greatest moves not, the dread of death.
Hence their warrior's heart hurls them against the steel, hence their
ready welcome of death.'[3]

'It was possibly the inculcation of these doctrines that moved the
Celtic warriors to hurl their bodies against cold steel – a character-
istic the world is only too familiar with in the conduct of our
Highland regiments. They can still listen to the battle-songs of a
thousand ages, with a susceptible mood nowise estranged amid the
crumbling foundations of a former sovereignty. A German military
authority – Clausewitz, I think – said that the Highlander is the
only soldier in Europe who, without training, can unflinchingly
face the bayonet.'

For now I see Life and Death as who gets
The first magical glimpse of Popocatepetl,

Its white cone floating in the rare winter air,
Incredibly near, . . . incredibly unreal,
And its sister peak which the Indians call
'The sleeping woman,' like a great prone goddess,
Above her circlet of clouds,
Or like Mount Elbruz's mile-apart twin breasts of snow!

I don't look the kind of guy, do I,
Who aches to get away from the high truth
Of the passing mountains into the close heat
Of the Pullman again, and the company of his pals
– Into a small enclosed space where I can feel
Confident and important again?
I am accustomed to the *altura*, believe me.
I am what the guides call *schwindelfrei*.

This is not the poetry of a man with such a grudge against life
That a very little of it goes a long way with him.
No great barbaric country will undermine and ruin me,
Slowly corroding my simple unimaginative qualities,
Rob me of my conventions, of my simple direct standards,
Who have no undefeatable inner integrity to take their place.
I love this country passionately, expanding
To its wild immensity as a flower opens in the sunshine,
I am the last man in all the world to hate these great places
And depend for my only comfort on the theatres and cafés,
The wide, well-lit *avenidas*, the scandal and gossip of the cabarets,
The emotion and danger of the bull-ring.
I would not rather be sitting in the closed comfort of the
    Pullman,
A drink before me, surrounded by people I know,
And things I can understand.

I feel with Life
As a man might towards a little child,
But towards Death, as towards one of my own contemporaries
Whom I have known as long
As I have known myself.

1 Rainer Maria Rilke.
2 Tio Nakamura.
3 Lucan, *Pharsalia*.

The Wund an' the Wetter

A Northumbrian Poem

Aah can mind the time when the men wad stand
On the top a the bank lookin' oot for' the land,
An' the sound a theer crack was as good as a sang
For' Langoth an' Collith t' Comely Carr,
For' the Bus a' the born t' the Shad an' the Bar,
Faggot, the Styenny Hyels, Fiddler's Fyace,
The Cock Craa' Stoene an' thon hob-hard place
At Herrod's Hoose Plantin on Aa'd Weir's hur;
The Chorch on the Black Rock, wheer ye shoot
Sooth for' the smooth at the Benty Gut;
T' the Cundy Rock an' the trink i' the sand
Reight ablow Featherblaa' – by, she was grand.
Ye could listen aa' neet. Th' wore spells, them words –
The map an' the key tae the treasure hoard.
Noo gi' us the marks for t' finnd 'em ageyn;
Howway doon t' the chorchyard an' ask the aa'd men,

For it's come wi' the wund an' gan wi' the wetter–
We'll noe be wantin' 'em noo . . .

But t' heor 'em gollerin' ower a boat
Wi' the soonds a the Norsemen still thick i' theer throat –
For' carlin t' fishrooms, inwaver t' crook,
Ye'll nivvor finnd these i' the page on a beuk –
Ah, but they're bonny, the pairts on a cowble –
Dip a' the forefoot, lang i' the scorbel,
For' tack heuk an' gripe t' the horns a' hor scut,
For' hor thofts t' hor thowelds – th' had nyems for the lot
That unlocked a hyel world' . . .

                          – Which is no t' forgit
The fagarrashin foond in a fisherman's hut –
(Ye'd say it could dae wi' a reight reed up!) –
Wi' pellets an' dookas an' pickets an' poys,
Swulls an' sweels an' bows for buoys,
Rowells an' bowelts an' barky sneyds,
The tyeble aa' claed wi' perrins a' threed,
Wi' hoppin's an' hingin's tha's toozled like tows,
An' pokes for the whullicks, an' bundles a skowbs,
An' bloots for' a dopper the caaldies ha' chowed.

But hey – look oot! – divvin't gan in theer:
Ye'll nivvor git lowswe, 'cos she's wizenbank fair!

It aa' tummels oot in a roosty shoower;
The nets unraffle wi' cloods a stoor.
Ye're varnigh scumfished afore ye can caal
For the becket, the brailer, the ripper an' aa'
The whuppin's an' leashin's aback a the waa' –
By, lad, she's a reight Taggarine-man's haal!

An' it's nae bother – it's naen
T' shut the door on yon.
Put oot the light. Forgit the nyems,
We'll nivvor be wantin' them things ageyn –
It's come wi' the wund an' gan wi' the wetter –
We'll noe be needin' 'em noo . . .

The Last Chantey

'And there was no more sea.'

Thus said the Lord in the Vault above the Cherubìm,
  Calling to the Angels and the Souls in their degree:
    'Lo! Earth has passed away
    On the smoke of Judgment Day.
  That Our word may be established shall We gather up the sea?'

Loud sang the souls of the jolly, jolly mariners:
  'Plague upon the hurricane that made us furl and flee!
    But the war is done between us,
    In the deep the Lord hath seen us –
  Our bones we'll leave the barracout', and God may sink the sea!'

Then said the soul of Judas that betrayèd Him:
  'Lord, hast Thou forgotten Thy covenant with me?
    How once a year I go
    To cool me on the floe?
  And Ye take my day of mercy if Ye take away the sea.'

Then said the soul of the Angel of the Off-shore Wind:
  (He that bits the thunder when the bull-mouthed breakers
      flee):
    'I have watch and ward to keep
    O'er Thy wonders on the deep,
  And Ye take mine honour from me if Ye take away the sea!'

Loud sang the souls of the jolly, jolly mariners:
  'Nay, but we were angry, and a hasty folk are we.
    If we worked the ship together
    Till she foundered in foul weather,
  Are we babes that we should clamour for a vengeance on
      the sea?'

Then said the souls of the slaves that men threw overboard:
  'Kennelled in the picaroon a weary band were we;
    But Thy arm was strong to save,
    And it touched us on the wave,
  And we drowsed the long tides idle till Thy Trumpets tore
      the sea.'

Then cried the soul of the stout Apostle Paul to God:
  'Once we frapped a ship, and she laboured woundily.
    There were fourteen score of these,
    And they blessed Thee on their knees,
  When they learned Thy Grace and Glory under Malta by
      the sea!'

Loud sang the souls of the jolly, jolly mariners,
  Plucking at their harps, and they plucked unhandily:
    'Our thumbs are rough and tarred,
    And the tune is something hard –
  May we lift a Deepsea Chantey such as seamen use at sea?'

Then said the souls of the gentlemen-adventurers –
  Fettered wrist to bar all for red iniquity:
    'Ho, we revel in our chains
    O'er the sorrow that was Spain's!
  Heave or sink it, leave or drink it, we were masters of the sea!'

Up spake the soul of a grey Gothavn 'speckshioner –
  (He that led the flenching in the fleets of fair Dundee):
    'Oh, the ice-blink white and near,
    And the bowhead breaching clear!
  Will Ye whelm them all for wantonness that wallow in the sea?'

Loud sang the souls of the jolly, jolly mariners,
  Crying: 'Under Heaven, here is neither lead nor lee!
    Must we sing for evermore

On the windless, glassy floor?
Take back your golden fiddles and we'll beat to open sea!'

Then stooped the Lord and He called the good sea up to Him,
And 'stablishèd its borders unto all eternity,
That such as have no pleasure
For to praise the Lord by measure,
They may enter into galleons and serve Him on the sea.

Sun, Wind, and Cloud shall fail not from the face of it,
Stinging, ringing spindrift, nor the fulmar flying free;
And the ships shall go abroad
To the Glory of the Lord
Who heard the silly sailor-folk and gave them back their sea!

The Hurricane

Lo, Lord, Thou ridest!
Lord, Lord, Thy swifting heart

Nought stayeth, nought now bideth
But's smithereened apart!

Ay! Scripture flee'th stone!
Milk-bright, Thy chisel wind

Rescindeth flesh from bone
To quivering whittlings thinned –

Swept, whistling straw! Battered,
Lord, e'en boulders now outleap

Rock sockets, levin-lathered!
Nor, Lord, may worm outdeep

Thy drum's gambade, its plunge abscond!
Lord God, while summits crashing

Whip sea-kelp screaming on blond
Sky-seethe, dense heaven dashing –

Thou ridest to the door, Lord!
Thou bidest wall nor floor, Lord!

'There came a Wind like a Bugle'

There came a Wind like a Bugle –
It quivered through the Grass
And a Green Chill upon the Heat
So ominous did pass
We barred the Windows and the Doors
As from an Emerald Ghost –
The Doom's electric Moccasin
That very instant passed –
On a strange Mob of panting Trees
And Fences fled away
And Rivers where the Houses ran
Those looked that lived – that Day –
The Bell within the steeple wild
The flying tidings told –
How much can come
And much can go,
And yet abide the World!

Chamber Music XXXV

All day I hear the noise of waters
       Making moan,
Sad as the seabird is when going
       Forth alone
He hears the winds cry to the waters'
       Monotone.

The grey winds, the cold winds are blowing
       Where I go.
I hear the noise of many waters
       Far below.
All day, all night, I hear them flowing
       To and fro.

The Frigate Pelican

Rapidly cruising or lying on the air there is a bird
    that realizes Rasselas's friend's project
    of wings uniting levity with strength. This
        hell-diver, frigate bird, hurricane-
bird; unless swift is the proper word
        for him, the storm omen when
    he flies close to the waves, should be seen
        fishing, although oftener
        he appears to prefer

to take, on the wing, from industrious crude-winged species,
    the fish they have caught, and is seldom successless.
    A marvel of grace, no matter how fast his
        victim may fly or how often may
turn. The others with similar ease,
    slowly rising once more,
        move out to the top
        of the circle and stop

and blow back, allowing the wind to reverse their direction –
    unlike the more stalwart swan that can ferry the
    woodcutter's two children home. Make hay; keep
        the shop; I have one sheep; were a less
limber animal's mottoes. This one
        finds sticks for the swan's-down dress
of his child to rest upon and would
        not know Gretel from Hänsel.
        As impassioned Handel –

meant for a lawyer and a masculine German domestic
    career – clandestinely studied the harpsichord
    and never was known to have fallen in love,
        the unconfiding frigate bird hides

in the height and in the majestic
        display of his art. He glides
    a hundred feet or quivers about
        as charred paper behaves – full
        of feints; and an eagle

of vigilance . . . *Festina lente*. Be gay
    civilly? How so? 'If I do well I am blessed
    whether any bless me or not, and if I do
        ill I am cursed.' We watch the moon rise
on the Susquehanna. In his way,
        this most romantic bird flies
to a more mundane place, the mangrove
        swamp to sleep. He wastes the moon.
        But he, and others, soon

rise from the bough and though flying, are able to foil the tired
    moment of danger that lays on heart and lungs the
    weight of the python that crushes to powder.

Over Sir John's Hill

Over Sir John's hill,
The hawk on fire hangs still;
In a hoisted cloud, at drop of dusk, he pulls to his claws
And gallows, up the rays of his eyes the small birds of the bay
And the shrill child's play
Wars
Of the sparrows and such who swansing, dusk, in wrangling
    hedges.
And blithely they squawk
To fiery tyburn over the wrestle of elms until
The flash the noosed hawk
Crashes, and slowly the fishing holy stalking heron
In the river Towy below bows his tilted headstone.

Flash, and the plumes crack,
And a black cap of jack-
Daws Sir John's just hill dons, and again the gulled birds hare
To the hawk on fire, the halter height, over Towy's fins,
In a whack of wind.
There
Where the elegiac fisherbird stabs and paddles
In the pebbly dab-filled
Shallow and sedge, and 'dilly dilly,' calls the loft hawk,
'Come and be killed,'
I open the leaves of the water at a passage
Of psalms and shadows among the pincered sandcrabs prancing
And read, in a shell,
Death clear as a buoy's bell:
All praise of the hawk on fire in hawk-eyed dusk be sung,
When his viperish fuse hangs looped with flames under the brand
Wing, and blest shall

Young
Green chickens of the bay and bushes cluck, 'dilly dilly,
Come let us die.'
We grieve as the blithe birds, never again, leave shingle and elm,
The heron and I,
I young Aesop fabling to the near night by the dingle
Of eels, saint heron hymning in the shell-hung distant

Crystal harbour vale
Where the sea cobbles sail,
And wharves of water where the walls dance and the white cranes
    stilt.
It is the heron and I, under judging Sir John's elmed
Hill, tell-tale the knelled
Guilt
Of the led-astray birds whom God, for their breast of whistles,
Have mercy on,
God in his whirlwind silence save, who marks the sparrows hail,
For their souls' song.
Now the heron grieves in the weeded verge. Through windows
Of dusk and water I see the tilting whispering
Heron, mirrored, go,
As the snapt feathers snow,
Fishing in the tear of the Towy. Only a hoot owl
Hollows, a grassblade blown in cupped hands, in the looted elms
And no green cocks or hens
Shout
Now on Sir John's hill. The heron, ankling the scaly
Lowlands of the waves,
Makes all the music; and I who hear the tune of the slow,
Wear-willow river, grave,
Before the lunge of the night, the notes on this time-shaken
Stone for the sake of the souls of the slain birds sailing.

The Falconer

[*from* Polyolbion]

When making for the brooke, the falkoner doth espie
On river, plash, or mere, where store of fowle doth lye:
Whence forced over land, by skilfull falconers trade:
A faire convenient flight, may easily be made.
He whistleth off his hawkes, whose nimble pineons streight,
Doe worke themselves by turnes, into a stately height:
And if that after check, the one or both doe goe,
Sometimes he them the lure, sometimes doth water show;
The trembling fowle that heare the jigging hawk-bels ring,
And find it is too late, to trust then to their wing,
Lye flat upon the flood, whilst the high-mounted hawks,
Then being lords alone, in their etheriall walkes,
Aloft so bravely stirre, their bells so thicke that shake;
Which when the falkoner sees, that scarce one plane they make:
The gallant'st birds saith he, that ever flew on wing,
And sweares there is a flight, were worthy of a King.

   Then making to the flood, to force the fowles to rise,
The fierce and eager hawkes, downe thrilling from the skies,
Make sundry canceleers e'r they the fowle can reach,
Which then to save their lives, their wings doe lively stretch.
But when the whizzing bels the silent ayre doe cleave,
And that their greatest speed, them vainly doe deceive;
And the sharpe cruell hawkes, they at their backs doe view,
Themselves for very feare they instantly ineawe.

   The hawkes get up againe into their former place;
And ranging here and there, in that their ayery race:
Still as the fearefull fowle attempt to scape away,
With many a stouping brave, them in againe they lay.
But when the falkoners take their hawking-poles in hand,

And crossing of the brooke, doe put it over land:
The hawke gives it a souse, that makes it to rebound,
Well neere the height of man, sometime above the ground;
Oft takes a leg, or wing, oft takes away the head,
And oft from necke to tayle, the backe in two doth shread.
With many a wo ho ho, and jocond lure againe,
When he his quarry makes upon the grassy plaine.

To Paint the Portrait of a Bird

for Elsa Henriquez

First of all paint a cage
Its door standing open
then paint
something appealing
something shining
something beautiful
something tasty
for the bird
then lean the canvas up against a tree
in a garden
in a forest
or in the woods
find another tree and hide yourself behind it
silently
without moving a muscle . . .
Sometimes the bird will come right away
but it could also take many long years
before it decides to.
Don't become discouraged
but wait
wait if you have to year after year after year
the earliness or lateness of its arrival has no relation
to the success of the work
When the bird appears
if he appears
maintain the most total silence
while you wait for the bird to enter the cage
and once he's in
softly shut the door with a quick stroke of your paintbrush

then
one by one blot out all the bars of the cage
taking care not to touch the bird's feathers
Then paint the tree's portrait
choosing the most beautiful of all its branches
for the bird
also paint the green foliage and the freshness of the breeze
the dust afloat in the sunlight
and the noises of the insects in the grass in the intense heat of
    summer
and then wait for the bird to sing
If the bird does not sing
it's a bad sign
a sign that the picture is bad
but if it does sing that's a good sign
that is to say a sign that you can sign
Then you reach out and gently pluck
one of the feathers of the bird
and you write your name over in one corner of the picture.

Translated from the French
by Michael Benedikt

The Emerald Dove

We ought to hang cutout hawk shapes
in our windows. Birds hard driven
by a predator, or maddened by a mirrored rival
too often die zonk against the panes'
invisible sheer, or stagger away from
the blind full stop in the air.
It was different with the emerald dove.
In at an open sash, a pair

sheered, missile, in a punch of energy,
one jinking on through farther doors, one
thrown, panicked by that rectangular wrong copse, braked
like a bullet in blood, a full-on splat of wings
like a vaulter between shoulders, blazed and calliper,
ashriek out of jagbeaked fixe fury, swatting wind,
lights, keepsakes, panes, then at the in window out, gone.
A sparrowhawk, by the cirrus feathering.

The other, tracked down in a farther room
clinging to a bedhead, was the emerald dove,
a rainforest bird, flashed in beyond its world
of lice, sudden death and tree seeds. Pigeon-like,
only its eye and neck in liquid motion,
there, as much beyond us as beyond
itself, it perched, barefoot in silks
like a prince of Sukhothai, above the reading lamps and
    cotton-buds.

Modest-sized as a writing hand, mushroom fawn
apart from its paua casque, those viridescent closed wings,
it was an emerald Levite in that bedroom

which the memory of it was going to bless for years
despite topping our ordinary happiness, as beauty
makes background of all around it. Levite too
in the question it posed: sanctuary without transformation,
which is, how we might be,

plunged out of our contentment into evolved strange heaven,
where the need to own or mate with or eat the beautiful
was bygone as poverty,
and we were incomprehensibly, in our exhaustion,
treasured, cooed at, then softly left alone
among vast crumples, verticals, refracting air,
our way home barred by mirrors, our splendour unmanifest
to us now, a small wild person, with no idea of peace.

Transcription of a Nightingale's Song

Chee chew chee chew chee
chew – cheer cheer cheer
chew chew chew chee
– up cheer up cheer up
tweet tweet tweet jug jug jug

wew wew wew – chur chur
woo it woo it tweet tweet
tweet jug jug jug

tee rew tee rew tee rew – gur
gur – chew rit chew rit – chur-chur chur
chur will-will will-will tweet-em
tweet em jug jug jug jug

grig grig grig chew chew

wevy wit wevy wit
wevy wit – chee-chit
chee-chit chee chit
weewit weewit wee
wit cheer cheer
cheer – pelew
pelew pelew –
bring a jug bring a
jug bring a jug

Crow's Ditty

Gowa! Gowa!
Wheea teea? Wheea teea?
Bagby Moor, Bagby Moor.
What ti dea there? What ti dea there?
Seek an au'd yeo, seek an au'd yeo.
Is she fat? Is she fat?
Gloor! Gloor! Gloor!

ANONYMOUS

Two Anchor Songs

1

Heisa, heisa,
Vorsa, vorsa,
Vou, vou,
One long pull,
More power,
Young blood,
More mud.

2

Vayra, veyra, vayra, veyra,
Gentil gallantis veynde;
I see hym, veynde, I see hym,
Porbossa, porbossa,
Hail all and ane, hail all and ane;
Hail hym up til us,
Hail hym up til us.

The Seafarer

May I for my own self song's truth reckon,
Journey's jargon, how I in harsh days
Hardship endured oft.
Bitter breast-cares have I abided,
Known on my keel many a care's hold,
And dire sea-surge, and there I oft spent
Narrow nightwatch nigh the ship's head
While she tossed close to cliffs. Coldly afflicted,
My feet were by frost benumbed.
Chill its chains are; chafing sighs
Hew my heart round and hunger begot
Mere-weary mood. Lest man know not
That he on dry land loveliest liveth,
List how I, care-wretched, on ice-cold sea,
Weathered the winter, wretched outcast
Deprived of my kinsmen;
Hung with hard ice-flakes, where hail-scur flew,
There I heard naught save the harsh sea
And ice-cold wave, at whiles the swan cries,
Did for my games the gannet's clamour,
Sea-fowls' loudness was for me laughter,
The mews' singing all my mead-drink.
Storms, on the stone-cliffs beaten, fell on the stern
In icy feathers; full oft the eagle screamed
With spray on his pinion.
        Not any protector
May make merry man faring needy.
This he little believes, who aye in winsome life
Abides 'mid burghers some heavy business,
Wealthy and wine-flushed, how I weary oft

Must bide above brine.
Neareth nightshade, snoweth from north,
Frost froze the land, hail fell on earth then,
Corn of the coldest. Nathless there knocketh now
The heart's thought that I on high streams
The salt-wavy tumult traverse alone.
Moaneth alway my mind's lust
That I fare forth, that I afar hence
Seek out a foreign fastness.
For this there's no mood-lofty man over earth's midst,
Not though he be given his good, but will have in his youth greed;
Nor his deed to the daring, nor his king to the faithful
But shall have his sorrow for sea-fare
Whatever his lord will.
He hath not heart for harping, nor in ring-having
Nor winsomeness to wife, nor world's delight
Nor any whit else save the wave's slash,
Yet longing comes upon him to fare forth on the water.
Bosque taketh blossom, cometh beauty of berries,
Fields to fairness, land fares brisker,
All this admonisheth man eager of mood,
The heart turns to travel so that he then thinks
On flood-ways to be far departing.
Cuckoo calleth with gloomy crying,
He singeth summerward, bodeth sorrow,
The bitter heart's blood. Burgher knows not –
He the prosperous man – what some perform
Where wandering them widest draweth.
So that but now my heart burst from my breastlock,
My mood 'mid the mere-flood,
Over the whale's acre, would wander wide.
On earth's shelter cometh oft to me,
Eager and ready, the crying lone-flyer,

Whets for the whale-path the heart irresistibly,
O'er tracks of ocean; seeing that anyhow
My lord deems to me this dead life
On loan and on land, I believe not
That any earth-weal eternal standeth
Save there be somewhat calamitous
That, ere a man's tide go, turn it to twain.
Disease or oldness or sword-hate
Beats out the breath from doom-gripped body.
And for this, every earl whatever, for those speaking after –
Laud of the living, boasteth some last word,
That he will work ere he pass onward,
Frame on the fair earth 'gainst foes his malice,
Daring ado, . . .
So that all men shall honour him after
And his laud beyond them remain 'mid the English,
Aye, for ever, a lasting life's-blast,
Delight 'mid the doughty.
                              Days little durable,
And all arrogance of earthen riches,
There come now no kings nor Caesars
Nor gold-giving lords like those gone.
Howe'er in mirth most magnified,
Whoe'er lived in life most lordliest,
Drear all this excellence, delights undurable!
Waneth the watch, but the world holdeth.
Tomb hideth trouble. The blade is layed low.
Earthly glory ageth and seareth.
No man at all going the earth's gait,
But age fares against him, his face paleth,
Grey-haired he groaneth, knows gone companions,
Lordly men, are to earth o'ergiven,
Nor may he then the flesh-cover, whose life ceaseth,

Nor eat the sweet nor feel the sorry,
Nor stir hand nor think in mid heart,
And though he strew the grave with gold,
His born brothers, their buried bodies
Be an unlikely treasure hoard.

Translated from the Anglo-Saxon
by Ezra Pound

Boat of a Million Years

The boat of a million years,
    boat of morning,
sails between the sycamores of turquoise,

Dawn white Dutch freighter
in the Red Sea – with a red stack –
heads past our tanker, out toward Ras Tanura,
    sun already fries my shoulder blades, I
    kneel on ragged steel decks chipping paint.
grey old T2 tanker and a
    white Dutch freighter,

    boat of the sun,
the abt-fish, the yut-fish,
    playing in the waves before it,

salty Red Sea
    dolphins rip sunlight
streak in, swirl and tangle
    under the forward arching wave-roll
of the cleaving bow

Teilhard said 'seize the tiller of the planet' he was joking,

We are led by dolphins toward morning.

Blow the Man Down

1. I'll sing ye a song o' the fish o' the sea,
     Chorus: Come all ye young sailormen, listen to me,
   An' I trust that ye'll join in the chorus with me.
     Chorus: I'll sing ye a song o' the fish o' the sea.

2. There wuz once an old skipper, I don't know his name,
   But I know that he once played a ruddy smart game.

3. When his ship lay becalmed in a tropical sea,
   He whistled all day but he could get no breeze.

4. But a seal heard his whistle an' loudly did call,
   'Just stow yer light canvas, jib, spanker, an' all.

5. I'll send ye some fish to consult if ye please,
   The best way to get ye a nice whistling breeze.'

6. Oh, first came the herring, sayin', 'I'm King o' the Seas',
   He jumped on the poop: 'Oh, the Capen I'll be!'

7. Next came the flatfish, they call him a skate:
   'If ye'll be the capen, why then I'm the mate.'

8. Then next came the hake, he wuz black as a rook,
   Sez he, 'I'm no sailor, I'll ship as the cook.'

9. Next came the shark with his two rows of teeth,
   'Cook, mind you the cabbage, an' I'll mind the beef!'

10. Then came the eel with his slippery tail,
    He climbed up aloft an' he cast off each sail.

11. Next came the codfish with his chuckle-head,
    He jumped in the chains an' began heavin' the lead.

12. Next came the flounder that lies on the ground,
    Sayin', 'Damn yer eyes, chucklehead, mind how ye sound!'

13. Then came the conger, as long as a mile,
    He gave a broad grin an' continued to smile.

14. Then came the porpoise with his pointed snout,
    He went to the wheel shoutin', 'Ready about!'

15. Then came the mackerel with his pretty striped back,
    He hauled aft each sheet, an' he boarded each tack.

16. Then came the whale, the biggest in the sea,
    Shoutin', 'Haul in yer head sheets, now, hellums a lee!'

17. Then came the sprat, he wuz smallest o' all,
    He jumped on the poop cryin', 'Maintawps'l haul!'

18. The mackerel the skipper did scoff for his tea,
    The herring he salted, the seal harpooned he.

19. He baited a hook, an' he thought it a lark,
    To catch as he did that hoary ol' shark.

20. The eel it wuz tasty, the hake it wuz strong,
    The flounder he speared with a lance o' three prongs.

21. The skate he speared next, but the porpose wuz fast,
    The conger it grinned an' it grinned to the last.

22. He caught the ol' whale, which wuz no simple task,
    An' soon with whale-oil he had filled up each cask.

23. With the head o' the codfish he made a fine pipe,
    The sprat then he salted, but 'twas only a bite.

24. The breeze it blew merrily, an' merrily sailed he,
    But what an' ol' barstard that skipper must be!

Fish

Fish, oh Fish,
So little matters!

Whether the waters rise and cover the earth
Or whether the waters wilt in the hollow places,
All one to you.

Aqueous, subaqueous,
Submerged
And wave-thrilled.

As the waters roll
Roll you.
The waters wash,
You wash in oneness
And never emerge.

Never know,
Never grasp.

Your life a sluice of sensation along your sides,
A flush at the flails of your fins, down the whorl of your tail,
And water wetly on fire in the grates of your gills;
Fixed water-eyes.

Even snakes lie together.

But oh, fish, that rock in water,
You lie only with the waters;
One touch.
No fingers, no hands and feet, no lips;
No tender muzzles,
No wistful bellies,

No loins of desire,
None.

You and the naked element,
Sway-wave.
Curvetting bits of tin in the evening light.

Who is it ejects his sperm to the naked flood?
In the wave-mother?
Who swims enwombed?
Who lies with the waters of his silent passion, womb-element?
– Fish in the waters under the earth.

What price *his* bread upon the waters?

Himself, all silvery himself
In the element,
No more.

Nothing more.

Himself,
And the element.
Food, of course!
Water-eager eyes,
Mouth-gate open
And strong spine urging, driving;
And desirous belly gulping.

Fear also!
He knows fear!
Water-eyes craning,
A rush that almost screams,
Almost fish-voice
As the pike comes . . .
Then gay fear, that turns the tail sprightly, from a shadow.

Food, and fear, and joie de vivre,
Without love.

The other way about:
Joie de vivre, and fear, and food,
All without love.

Quelle joie de vivre
Dans l'eau!
Slowly to gape through the waters,
Alone with the element;
To sink, and rise, and go to sleep with the waters;
To speak endless inaudible wavelets into the wave;
To breathe from the flood at the gills,
Fish-blood slowly running next to the flood, extracting fish-fire;
To have the element under one, like a lover;
And to spring away with a curvetting click in the air,
Provocative.
Dropping back with a slap on the face of the flood.
And merging oneself!

To be a fish!

So utterly without misgiving
To be a fish
In the waters.

Loveless, and so lively!
Born before God was love,
Or life knew loving.
Beautifully beforehand with it all.

Admitted, they swarm in companies,
Fishes.
They drive in shoals.
But soundless, and out of contact.

They exchange no word, no spasm, not even anger.
Not one touch.
Many suspended together, forever apart,
Each one alone with the waters, upon one wave with the rest.

A magnetism in the water between them only.

I saw a water-serpent swim across the Anapo,
And I said to my heart, *look, look at him!*
With his head up, steering like a bird!
He's a rare one, but he belongs . . .

But sitting in a boat on the Zeller lake
And watching the fishes in the breathing waters
Lift and swim and go their way –

I said to my heart, *who are these?*
And my heart couldn't own them . . .
A slim young pike, with smart fins
And grey-striped suit, a young cub of a pike
Slouching along away below, half out of sight,
Like a lout on an obscure pavement . . .

Aha, there's somebody in the know!

But watching closer
That motionless deadly motion,
That unnatural barrel body, that long ghoul nose, . . .
I left off hailing him.

I had made a mistake, I didn't know him,
This grey, monotonous soul in the water,
This intense individual in shadow,
Fish-alive.

I didn't know his God.
I didn't know his God.

Which is perhaps the last admission that life has to wring
    out of us.

I saw, dimly,
Once a big pike rush,
And small fish fly like splinters.
And I said to my heart, *there are limits*
To you, my heart;
And to the one God.
Fish are beyond me.

Other Gods
Beyond my range . . . gods beyond my God . . .

They are beyond me, are fishes.
I stand at the pale of my being
And look beyond, and see
Fish, in the outerwards,
As one stands on a bank and looks in.

I have waited with a long rod
And suddenly pulled a gold-and-greenish, lucent fish from below,
And had him fly like a halo round my head,
Lunging in the air on the line.

Unhooked his gorping, water-honey mouth,
And seen his horror-tilted eye,
His red-gold, water-precious, mirror-flat bright eye;
And felt him beat in my hand, with his mucous, leaping life-throb.
And my heart accused itself
Thinking: *I am not the measure of creation.*
This is beyond me, this fish.
His God stands outside my God.

And the gold-and-green pure lacquer-mucus comes off
    in my hand,

And the red-gold mirror-eye stares and dies,
And the water-suave contour dims.

But not before I have had to know
He was born in front of my sunrise,
Before my day.

He outstarts me.
And I, a many-fingered horror of daylight to him,
Have made him die.

Fishes
With their gold, red eyes, and green-pure gleam, and undergold,
And their pre-world loneliness,
And more-than-lovelessness,
And white meat;
They move in other circles.
Outsiders.
Water-wayfarers.
Things of one element.
Aqueous,
Each by itself.

Cats, and the Neapolitans,
Sulphur sun-beasts,
Thirst for fish as for more-than-water;
Water-alive
To quench their over-sulphureous lusts.

But I, I only wonder
And don't know.
I don't know fishes.

In the beginning
Jesus was called The Fish . . .
And in the end.

The Ancients of the World

The salmon lying in the depths of Llyn Llifon,
    Secretly as a thought in a dark mind,
Is not so old as the owl of Cwm Cowlyd
    Who tells her sorrow nightly on the wind.

The ousel singing in the woods of Cilgwri,
    Tirelessly as a stream over the mossed stones,
Is not so old as the toad of Cors Fochno
    Who feels the cold skin sagging round his bones.

The toad and the ousel and the stag of Rhedynfre,
    That has cropped each leaf from the tree of life,
Are not so old as the owl of Cwm Cowlyd,
    That the proud eagle would have to wife.

The Eighth Elegy

Dedicated to Rudolf Kassner

With all its eyes the natural world looks out
into the Open. Only *our* eyes are turned
backward, and surround plant, animal, child
like traps, as they emerge into their freedom.
We know what is really out there only from
the animal's gaze; for we take the very young
child and force it around, so that it sees
objects – not the Open, which is so
deep in animals' faces. Free from death.
We, only, can see death; the free animal
has its decline in back of it, forever,
and God in front, and when it moves, it moves
already in eternity, like a fountain.

Never, not for a single day, do *we* have
before us that pure space into which flowers
endlessly open. Always there is World
and never Nowhere without the No: that pure
unseparated element which one breathes
without desire and endlessly *knows*. A child
may wander there for hours, through the timeless
stillness, may get lost in it and be
shaken back. Or someone dies and *is* it.
For, nearing death, one doesn't see death; but stares
beyond, perhaps with an animal's vast gaze.
Lovers, if the beloved were not there
blocking the view, are close to it, and marvel . . .
As if by some mistake, it opens for them
behind each other . . . But neither can move past
the other, and it changes back to World.

Forever turned toward objects, we see in them
the mere reflection of the realm of freedom,
which we have dimmed. Or when some animal
mutely, serenely, looks us through and through.
That is what fate means: to be opposite,
to be opposite and nothing else, forever.
If the animal moving toward us so securely
in a different direction had our kind of
consciousness –, it would wrench us around and drag us
along its path. But it feels its life as boundless,
unfathomable, and without regard
to its own condition: pure, like its outward gaze.
And where we see the future, it sees all time
and itself within all time, forever healed.

Yet in the alert, warm animal there lies
the pain and burden of an enormous sadness.
For it too feels the presence of what often
overwhelms us: a memory, as if
the element we keep pressing toward was once
more intimate, more true, and our communion
infinitely tender. Here all is distance;
there it was breath. After that first home,
the second seems ambiguous and drafty.
    Oh bliss of the *tiny* creature which remains
forever inside the womb that was its shelter;
joy of the gnat which, still *within*, leaps up
even at its marriage: for everything is womb.
And look at the half-assurance of the bird,
which knows both inner and outer, from its source,
as if it were the soul of an Etruscan,
flown out of a dead man received inside a space,
but with his reclining image as the lid.

And how bewildered is any womb-born creature
that has to fly. As if terrified and fleeing
from itself, it zigzags through the air, the way
a crack runs through a teacup. So the bat
quivers across the porcelain of evening.

And we: spectators, always, everywhere,
turned toward the world of objects, never outward.
It fills us. We arrange it. It breaks down.
We rearrange it, then break down ourselves.
Who has twisted us around like this, so that
no matter what we do, we are in the posture
of someone going away? Just as, upon
the farthest hill, which shows him his whole valley
one last time, he turns, stops, lingers–,
so we live here, forever taking leave.

Translated from the German
by Stephen Mitchell

from Folklore

One sommers when the soft sonne
Dressed in a shepherds shroud
Went wide in this world for wondres to hear

But on a May morning on the Malvern Hills
Fell into a vision.

The Vision of Piers Plowman

1

Man walks in to sky. A crows, muttering, didicoy.

Lays his feet in the rain. Tar paper peeling & waters form. (His) piss blades. The bramble hedge. Crawls through doors. Feathers fall over His black suit. Lies inside. His dark song.

In his heart he. Lifts the car off the farmer and ran. Tossed his bike in the hedge & wrestles a man down. Ate the flowers with his bare hands.

Rain & rain from the west and the clouds in the shape.

Where you from boy? He says he comes. Says he comes from the borders, boy. He says he comes from Eardisley. Where you from, boy? Where you from?

2

Breathes in the dry lights & dries him. Aspires towards dark.

All the quick animals. The angry the secretive ones.

What are their names? (What are their) marks?

3

When he stood up he knocked him back down and the cold.

All night in the lane in the hedgerow lays. Drinking.

His breath it comes out of the man like in sheets, like. Water frozen inside the boots. Sees starlings take sustenance from the earth and circle. Black things come. Before their eyes. (Walked for days.)

They cuts the small tree and they lays it down. In a line. Like a cut to the neck, half across. So the thing lives and clean. So it flowers. Birds inside too sometimes men. Found a man inside once sleeping. With snow on.

Feels the poplar with his teeth, and the birch. Makes its paper sweet. Where the tongue & black branches drip. Water percolates. The clear night is in. Stars burn. & waters burn. Watches the light behind the eyes.

Comes into us. Sleep. Sucking it down through a straw. The animals sleep. Dies. Every time.

Makes a hedgerow, thus.

4

Steals between the honeycomb wire and break their necks every one. Sees the cold dawn sees it coming up over Bredon's cold hill. Halfway up the nostrils and into fox lungs. Climbs it up and leaves a red stain on the hill side there.

Goes over the fields. Goes over the fields. Like,

To a Mouse

On turning her up in her nest with the plough, November 1785

Wee sleekit, cow'rin, tim'rous beastie,
O, what a panic's in thy breastie!
Thou need na start awa sae hasty,
      Wi bickering brattle!
I wad be laith to rin an chase thee,
      Wi murdering pattle!

I'm truly sorry man's dominion
Has broken Nature's social union,
An justifies that ill opinion,
      Which makes thee startle
At me, thy poor, earth-born companion,
      An fellow mortal!

I doubt na, whyles, but thou may thieve;
What then? poor beastie, thou maun live!
A daimen icker in a thrave
     'S a sma request;
I'll get a blessin wi the lave,
      An never miss't!

Thy wee-bit housie, too, in ruin!
Its silly wa's the win's are strewin!
An naething, now, to big a new ane,
      O foggage green!
An bleak December's win's ensuin,
      Baith snell an keen!

Thou saw the fields laid bare an waste,
An weary winter comin fast,
An cozie here, beneath the blast,

            Thou thought to dwell,
Till crash! the cruel coulter past
            Out thro thy cell.

That wee bit heap o leaves an stibble,
Has cost thee monie a' weary nibble!
Now thou's turn'd out, for a thy trouble,
            But house or hald,
To thole the winter's sleety dribble,
            An cranreuch cauld!

But Mousie, thou art no thy lane,
In proving foresight may be vain:
The best-laid schemes o mice an men
            Gang aft agley,
An lea'e us nought but grief an pain,
            For promis'd joy!

Still thou art blest, compar'd wi me!
The present only toucheth thee:
But och! I backward cast my e'e,
        On prospects drear!
An forward, tho I canna see,
        I guess an fear!

bickering brattle, scurrying rush; *pattle*, spade; *daimen icker in a thrave*, odd ear in
sheaves; *silly wa's*, feeble walls; *foggage*, coarse grass; *coulter*, ploughshare; *thole*,
endure; *cranreuch*, hoar-frost; *thy lane*, alone

[Transcribed from the verses of the Burnt Plain]
Aboriginal totem song

To the Westward it keeps on chirping
The cricket keeps on chirping
With sorrowful longing it keeps on chirping

To the westward it keeps on chirping
The cricket keeps on chirping
Over yonder it keeps on chirping . . .

In the Likeness of a Grasshopper

A trap
Waits on the field path.

A wicker contraption, with working parts,
Its spring tensed and set.

So flimsily made, out of grass
(Out of the stems, the joints, the raspy-dry flags).

Baited with a fur-soft caterpillar,
A belly of amorous life, pulsing signals.

Along comes a love-sick, perfume-footed
Music of the wild earth.

The trap, touched by a breath,
Jars into action, its parts blur –

And music cries out.

A sinewy violin
Has caught its violinist.

Cloud-fingered summer, the beautiful trapper,
Picks up the singing cage

And takes out the Song, adds it to the Songs
With which she robes herself, which are her wealth,

Sets her trap again, a yard further on.

'First of summer, lovely sight'

First of summer, lovely sight,
season of perfection!
At the slightest ray the sun sends
blackbirds sing their full song.

The hardy vigorous cuckoo calls
all hail to high summer.
The bitter weather is abated
when the branched woods were torn.

Summer dries the stream down small,
the swift herd searches for a pool.
Heather spreads its hair afar.
The pale bog-cotton, faint, flourishes.

Buds break out on the hawthorn bush.
The sea runs its calm course
– the salt sea the season soothes.
Blossom blankets the world.

Bees' feet, with tiny strength,
carry their bundles, sucked from blossom.
The hill-fields call to the cattle.
Ants are active in swarming plenty.

The woods' harp works its music;
the harmony brings total peace.
Dust blows out of all our houses,
haze blows from the brimming lake.

The sturdy corncrake-poet speaks.
The cold cataract calls its greeting
down to the warm pool from on high.
Rushes begin to rustle.

ANONYMOUS

Slim swallows flash on high:
living music rings the hill.
Moist fruits grow fat and heavy.
. . . the marsh . . .

. . . the lovely marsh:
grass in a fine, packed path.
The speckled fish makes a leap
at the swift fly – worthy warriors.

Man thrives: all things flourish.
The great slopes are full of gifts.
Each forest glade is shining bright
and bright each broad and lovely plain.

The whole season full of wonder:
Winter's harsh wind is gone.
The fruitful woods are fair.
Summer is a great ease.

A flock of birds settles to earth:
they have seen a woman there.*
The green field echoes
where a stream runs brisk and bright.

Horse riding; wild ardour;
ranked hosts ranged around.
Tree-white freed across the land,
giving up an iris-gold!

A delicate and timorous thing
is singing ceaseless in the air,
and rightly, from a full throat:
'First of summer, lovely sight!'

Translated from the Irish
by Thomas Kinsella

A Voice of Summer

In this one of all fields I know the best
All day and night, hoarse and melodious, sounded
A creeping corncrake, coloured like the ground,
Till the cats got him and gave the rough air rest.

Mechanical August, dowdy in the reeds,
He ground his quern and the round minutes sifted
Away in the powdery light. He would never lift
His beady periscope over the dusty hayseeds.

Cunning low-runner, tobogganing on his breast
He slid from sight once, from my feet. He only
Became the grass; then stone scraped harsh on stone,
Boxing the compass round his trivial nest.

– Summer now is diminished, is less by him.
Something that it could say cannot be spoken –
As though the language of a subtle folk
Had lost a word that had no synonym.

A Landscape Heard

Radio Sintesi

The whistle of a blackbird, envious of the crackling of a fire,
ends by extinguishing the gossip of water.

  10 seconds of lapping.
    1 second of crackling.
    8 seconds of lapping.
    1 second of crackling.
    5 seconds of lapping.
    1 second of crackling.
  19 seconds of lapping.
    1 second of crackling.
  25 seconds of lapping.
    1 second of crackling.
  35 seconds of lapping.
    6 seconds of the whistle of a blackbird.

Translated from the Italian
by Victoria Nes Kerby

Into the Dusk-charged Air

Far from the Rappahannock, the silent
Danube moves along toward the sea.
The brown and green Nile rolls slowly
Like the Niagara's welling descent.
Tractors stood on the green banks of the Loire
Near where it joined the Cher.
The St. Lawrence prods among black stones
And mud. But the Arno is all stones.
Wind ruffles the Hudson's
Surface. The Irawaddy is overflowing.
But the yellowish, gray Tiber
Is contained within steep banks. The Isar
Flows too fast to swim in, the Jordan's water
Courses over the flat land. The Allegheny and its boats
Were dark blue. The Moskowa is
Gray boats. The Amstel flows slowly.
Leaves fall into the Connecticut as it passes
Underneath. The Liffey is full of sewage,
Like the Seine, but unlike
The brownish-yellow Dordogne.
Mountains hem in the Colorado
And the Oder is very deep, almost
As deep as the Congo is wide.
The plain banks of the Neva are
Gray. The dark Saône flows silently.
And the Volga is long and wide
As it flows across the brownish land. The Ebro
Is blue, and slow. The Shannon flows
Swiftly between its banks. The Mississippi
Is one of the world's longest rivers, like the Amazon.

It has the Missouri for a tributary.
The Harlem flows amid factories
And buildings. The Nelson is in Canada,
Flowing. Through hard banks the Dubawnt
Forces its way. People walk near the Trent.
The landscape around the Mohawk stretches away;
The Rubicon is merely a brook.
In winter the Main
Surges; the Rhine sings its eternal song.
The Rhône slogs along through whitish banks
And the Rio Grande spins tales of the past.
The Loir bursts its frozen shackles
But the Moldau's wet mud ensnares it.
The East catches the light.
Near the Escaut the noise of factories echoes
And the sinuous Humboldt gurgles wildly.
The Po too flows, and the many-colored
Thames. Into the Atlantic Ocean
Pours the Garonne. Few ships navigate
On the Housatonic, but quite a few can be seen
On the Elbe. For centuries
The Afton has flowed.

                    If the Rio Negro
Could abandon its song, and the Magdalena
The jungle flowers, the Tagus
Would still flow serenely, and the Ohio
Abrade its slate banks. The tan Euphrates would
Sidle silently across the world. The Yukon
Was choked with ice, but the Susquehanna still pushed
Bravely along. The Dee caught the day's last flares
Like the Pilcomayo's carrion rose.
The Peace offered eternal fragrance
Perhaps, but the Mackenzie churned livid mud

Like tan chalk-marks. Near where
The Brahmaputra slapped swollen dikes
Was an opening through which the Limmat
Could have trickled. A young man strode the Churchill's
Banks, thinking of night. The Vistula seized
The shadows. The Theiss, stark mad, bubbled
In the windy evening. And the Ob shuffled
Crazily along. Fat billows encrusted the Dniester's
Pallid flood, and the Fraser's porous surface.
Fish gasped amid the Spree's reeds. A boat
Descended the bobbing Orinoco. When the
Marne flowed by the plants nodded
And above the glistering Gila
A sunset as beautiful as the Athabasca
Stammered. The Zambezi chimed. The Oxus
Flowed somewhere. The Paranaíba
Is flowing, like the wind-washed Cumberland.
The Araguaia flows in the rain.
And, through overlying rocks the Isère
Cascades gently. The Guadalquivir sputtered.
Someday time will confound the Indre,
Making a rill of the Huang Ho. And
The Potomac rumbles softly. Crested birds
Watch the Ucayali go
Through dreaming night. You cannot stop
The Yenisei. And afterwards
The White flows strongly to its . . .
Goal. If the Tyne's shores
Hold you, and the Albany
Arrest your development, can you resist the Red's
Musk, the Meuse's situation?
A particle of mud in the Neckar
Does not turn it black. You cannot

Like the Saskatchewan, nor refuse
The meandering Yangtze, unleash
The Genesee. Does the Scamander
Still irrigate crimson plains? And the Durance
And the Pechora? The São Francisco
Skulks amid gray, rubbery nettles. The Liard's
Reflexes are slow, and the Arkansas erodes
Anthracite hummocks. The Paraná stinks.
The Ottawa is light emerald green
Among grays. Better that the Indus fade
In steaming sands! Let the Brazos
Freeze solid! And the Wabash turn to a leaden
Cinder of ice! The Marañón is too tepid, we must
Find a way to freeze it hard. The Ural
Is freezing slowly in the blasts. The black Yonne
Congeals nicely. And the Petit-Morin
Curls up on the solid earth. The Inn
Does not remember better times, and the Merrimack's
Galvanized. The Ganges is liquid snow by now;
The Vyatka's ice-gray. The once-molten Tennessee's
Curdled. The Japurá is a pack of ice. Gelid
The Columbia's gray loam banks. The Don's merely
A giant icicle. The Niger freezes, slowly.
The interminable Lena plods on
But the Purus' mercurial waters are icy, grim
With cold. The Loing is choked with fragments of ice.
The Weser is frozen, like liquid air.
And so is the Kama. And the beige, thickly flowing
Tocantins. The rivers bask in the cold.
The stern Uruguay chafes its banks,
A mass of ice. The Hooghly is solid
Ice. The Adour is silent, motionless.
The lovely Tigris is nothing but scratchy ice

Like the Yellowstone, with its osier-clustered banks.
The Mekong is beginning to thaw out a little
And the Donets gurgles beneath the
Huge blocks of ice. The Manzanares gushes free.
The Illinois darts through the sunny air again.
But the Dnieper is still ice-bound. Somewhere
The Salado propels its floes, but the Roosevelt's
Frozen. The Oka is frozen solider
Than the Somme. The Minho slumbers
In winter, nor does the Snake
Remember August. Hilarious, the Canadian
Is solid ice. The Madeira slavers
Across the thawing fields, and the Plata laughs.
The Dvina soaks up the snow. The Sava's
Temperature is above freezing. The Avon
Carols noiselessly. The Drôme presses
Grass banks; the Adige's frozen
Surface is like gray pebbles.

Birds circle the Ticino. In winter
The Var was dark blue, unfrozen. The
Thwaite, cold, is choked with sandy ice;
The Ardèche glistens feebly through the freezing rain.

Nymphs of Rivers

[*From* Polyolbion]

Glico the running streames in sweetnesse still that keepes,
And Clymene which rules, when they surround their deepes.
Spio, in hollow bankes, the waters that doth hide:
With Opis that doth beare them backward with the tyde.
Semaia that for sights doth keepe the water cleare:
Zanthe their yellow sands, that maketh to appeare,
Then Drymo for the okes that shaddow every banke,
Phylodice, the boughs for garlands fresh and ranke.
Which the cleare Naiades make them anadems with all,
When they are cald to daunse in Neptunes mightie hall.
Then Ligea, which maintaines the birds harmonious layes,
Which sing on rivers banks amongst the slender sprayes,
With Rhodia, which for them doth nurse the roseat sets,
Ioida, which preserves the azure violets.
Anthea, of the flowers, that hath the generall charge,
And Syrinx of the reeds, that grow upon the marge,
Some of these lovely nymphes wore on their flaxen haire
Fine chaplets made of flaggs, that fully flowred were:
With water-cans againe, some wantonly them dight,
Whose larger leafe and flower, gave wonderfull delight
To those that wistly view'd their beauties: some againe,
That soveraigne places held amongst the watry traine,
Of cat-tayles made them crownes, which from the sedge doth grow,
Which neatly woven were, and some to grace the show,
Of lady-smocks most white, doe rob each neighbouring mead,
Wherewith their looser locks most curiously they breyd.

MICHAEL DRAYTON

Estuary

RUSH	SEDGE	COUCH	MARRAM	BENT
CURLEW	WHIMBREL	GULL	LAPWING	TERN
ESSO	MOBIL	BP	EXXON	SHELL

Canal Bank Walk

Leafy-with-love banks and the green waters of the canal
Pouring redemption for me, that I do
The will of God, wallow in the habitual, the banal,
Grow with nature again as before I grew.
The bright stick trapped, the breeze adding a third
Party to the couple kissing on an old seat,
And a bird gathering materials for the nest for the Word
Eloquently new and abandoned to its delirious beat.
O unworn world enrapture me, encapture me in a web
Of fabulous grass and eternal voices by a beech,
Feed the gaping need of my senses, give me ad lib
To pray unselfconsciously with overflowing speech
For this soul needs to be honoured with a new dress woven
From green and blue things and arguments that cannot be proven.

The Word

There are so many things I have forgot,
That once were much to me, or that were not,
All lost, as is a childless woman's child
And its child's children, in the undefiled
Abyss of what can never be again.
I have forgot, too, names of the mighty men
That fought and lost or won in the old wars,
Of kings and fiends and gods, and most of the stars.
Some things I have forgot that I forget.
But lesser things there are, remembered yet,
Than all the others. One name that I have not –
Though 'tis an empty thingless name – forgot
Never can die because Spring after Spring
Some thrushes learn to say it as they sing.
There is always one at midday saying it clear
And tart – the name, only the name I hear.
While perhaps I am thinking of the elder scent
That is like food, or while I am content
With the wild rose scent that is like memory,
This name suddenly is cried out to me
From somewhere in the bushes by a bird
Over and over again, a pure thrush word.

Riley

Down in the water-meadows Riley
Spread his wash on the bramble-thorn,
Sat, one foot in the moving water,
Bare as the day that he was born.

Candid was his curling whisker,
Brown his body as an old tree-limb,
Blue his eye as the jay above him
Watching him watch the minjies swim.

Four stout sticks for walls had Riley,
His roof was a rusty piece of tin,
As snug in the lew of a Cornish hedgerow
He watched the seasons out and in.

He paid no rates, he paid no taxes,
His lamp was the moon hung in the tree.
Though many an ache and pain had Riley
He envied neither you nor me.

Many a friend from bush or burrow
To Riley's hand would run or fly,
And soft he'd sing and sweet he'd whistle
Whatever the weather in the sky.

Till one winter's morning Riley
From the meadow vanished clean.
Gone was the rusty tin, the timber,
As if old Riley had never been.

What strange secret had old Riley?
Where did he come from? Where did he go?
Why was his heart as light as summer?
Never know now, said the jay. *Never know.*

minjies, small minnows; *lew*, lee

'There was a man of double deed'

There was a man of double deed
Sowed his garden full of seed.
When the seed began to grow,
'Twas like a garden full of snow;
When the snow began to melt,
'Twas like a ship without a belt;
When the ship began to sail,
'Twas like a bird without a tail;
When the bird began to fly
'Twas like an eagle in the sky;
When the sky began to roar,
'Twas like a lion at the door;
When the door began to crack,
'Twas like a stick across my back;
When my back began to smart,
'Twas like a penknife in my heart;
When my heart began to bleed,
'Twas death and death and death
indeed.

Putting in the Seed

You come to fetch me from my work tonight
When supper's on the table, and we'll see
If I can leave off burying the white
Soft petals fallen from the apple tree
(Soft petals, yes, but not so barren quite,
Mingled with these, smooth bean and wrinkled pea),
And go along with you ere you lose sight
Of what you came for and become like me,
Slave to a springtime passion for the earth.
How Love burns through the Putting in the Seed
On through the watching for that early birth
When, just as the soil tarnishes with weed,
The sturdy seedling with arched body comes
Shouldering its way and shedding the earth crumbs.

The Seed

Someone sows someone
Sows him in his head
Stamps the earth down well

Waits for the seed to sprout

The seed hollows out his head
Turns it into a mousehole
The mice eat the seed

They drop dead

The wind comes to live in the empty head
And gives birth to chequered breezes

Translated from the Serbo-Croat
by Anne Pennington

'Spring is like a perhaps hand'

Spring is like a perhaps hand
(which comes carefully
out of Nowhere)arranging
a window, into which people look(while
people stare
arranging and changing placing
carefully there a strange
thing and a known thing here)and

changing everything carefully

spring is like a perhaps
Hand in a window
(carefully to
and fro moving New and
Old things, while
people stare carefully
moving a perhaps
fraction of flower here placing
an inch of air there)and

without breaking anything.

Celebrations

Quhen Merche wes with variand windis past,
And Appryll had with hir silver schouris
Tane leif at Nature with one orient blast,
And lusty May that muddir is of flouris
Had maid the birdis to begyn thair houris
Amang the tendir odouris reid and quhyt,
Quhois armony to heir it wes delyt:

In bed at morrow, sleiping as I lay,
Me thocht Aurora with hir cristall ene
In at the window lukit by the day
And halsit me, with visage paill and grene;
On quhois hand a lark sang fro the splene,
'Awalk, luvaris, out of your slomering,
Se how the lusty morrow dois up spring.'

Me thocht fresche May befoir my bed upstude
In weid depaynt of mony divers hew,
Sobir, benyng, and full of mansuetude,
In brycht atteir of flouris forgit new,
Hevinly of color, quhyt, reid, broun and blew,
Balmit in dew, and gilt with Phebus bemys
Quhill all the hous illumynit of hir lemys.

'Slugird', scho said, 'awalk annone for schame,
And in my honour sum thing thow go wryt;
The lork hes done the mirry day proclame
To rais up luvaris with confort and delyt,
Yit nocht incresis thy curage to indyt,
Quhois hart sum tyme hes glaid and blisfull bene
Sangis to mak undir the levis grene.'

'Quhairto', quod I, 'sall I uprys at morrow?
For in this May few birdis herd I sing;
Thai haif moir caus to weip and plane thair sorrow,
Thy air it is nocht holsum nor benyng:
Lord Eolus dois in thy sessone ring;
So busteous ar the blastis of his horne,
Amang thy bewis to walk I haif forborne.'

With that this lady sobirly did smyll,
And said, 'Uprys and do thy observance;
Thow did promyt in Mayis lusty quhyle
For to discryve the Ros of most plesance.
Go se the birdis how thay sing and dance,
Illumynit our with orient skyis brycht,
Annamyllit richely with new asur lycht.'

Quhen this wes said, depairtit scho, this quene,
And enterit in a lusty gairding gent;
And than me thocht full hestely besene
In serk and mantill [eftir hir] I went
In to this garth, most dulce and redolent
Off herb and flour and tendir plantis sueit
And grene levis doing of dew doun fleit.

The purpour sone with tendir bemys reid
In orient bricht as angell did appeir,
Throw goldin skyis putting up his heid;
Quhois gilt tressis schone so wondir cleir
That all the world tuke confort, fer and neir,
To luke upone his fresche and blisfull face
Doing all sable fro the hevynnis chace.

And as the blisfull soune of cherarchy
The fowlis song throw confort of the licht:
The birdis did with oppin vocis cry,

'O luvaris fo, away, thow dully nycht,
And welcum day that confortis every wight;
Haill May, haill Flora, haill Aurora schene,
Haill princes Natur, haill Venus luvis quene.'

Dame Natur gaif ane inhibitioun thair
To fers Neptunus and Eolus the bawld,
Nocht to perturb the wattir nor the air;
And that no schouris nor blastis cawld
Effray suld flouris nor fowlis on the fold,
Scho bad eik Juno, goddes of the sky,
That scho the hevin suld keip amene and dry.

Scho ordand eik that every bird and beist
Befoir hir hienes suld annone compeir,
And every flour of vertew, most and leist,
And every herb be feild fer and neir,
As thay had wont in May fro yeir to yeir
To hir thair makar to mak obediens,
Full law inclynnand with all dew reverens.

With that annone scho send the swyft ro
To bring in beistis of all conditioun;
The restles suallow commandit scho also
To feche all fowll of small and greit renown;
And to gar flouris compeir of all fassoun
Full craftely conjurit scho the yarrow,
Quhilk did furth swirk als swift as ony arrow.

All present wer in twynkling of ane e,
Baith beist and bird and flour, befoir the quene:
And first the Lyone, gretast of degre,
Was callit thair, and he most fair to sene
With a full hardy contenance and kene
Befoir dame Natur come, and did inclyne
With visage bawld and curage leonyne.

This awfull beist full terrible wes of cheir,
Persing of luke and stout of countenance,
Rycht strong of corpis, of fassoun fair but feir,
Lusty of schaip, lycht of deliverance,
Reid of his cullour as is the ruby glance:
On feild of gold he stude full mychtely,
With flour delycis sirculit lustely.

This lady liftit up his cluvis cleir
And leit him listly lene upone hir kne,
And crownit him with dyademe full deir
Off radyous stonis, most ryall for to se,
Saying, 'The king of beistis mak I the,
And the cheif protector in woddis and schawis:
Onto thi leigis go furth, and keip the lawis.

Exerce justice with mercy and conscience,
And lat no small beist suffir skaith na skornis
Of greit beistis that bene of moir piscence;
Do law elyk to aipis and unicornis,
And lat no bowgle with his busteous hornis
The meik pluch ox oppress, for all his pryd,
Bot in the yok go peciable him besyd.'

Quhen this was said, with noyis and soun of joy
All kynd of beistis in to thair degre
At onis cryit lawd, 'Vive le Roy',
And till his feit fell with humilite;
And all thay maid him homege and fewte,
And he did thame ressaif with princely laitis,
Quhois noble yre is *parcere prostratis*.

Syne crownit scho the Egle king of fowlis,
And as steill dertis scherpit scho his pennis,
And bawd him be als just to awppis and owlis
As unto pacokkis, papingais, or crennis,

And mak a law for wycht fowlis and for wrennis;
And lat no fowll of ravyne do efferay,
Nor devoir birdis bot his awin pray.

Than callit scho all flouris that grew on feild,
Discirnyng all thair fassionis and effeiris;
Upon the awfull Thrissill scho beheld
And saw him kepit with a busche of speiris;
Concedring him so able for the weiris,
A radius croun of rubeis scho him gaif
And said, 'In feild go furth and fend the laif:

And sen thow art a king, thow be discreit;
Herb without vertew thow hald nocht of sic pryce
As herb of vertew and of odor sueit,
And lat no nettill vyle and full of vyce
Hir fallow to the gudly flour delyce,
Nor latt no wyld weid full of churlichenes
Compair hir till the lilleis nobilnes.

Nor hald non udir flour in sic denty
As the fresche Ros of cullour reid and quhyt;
For gife thow dois, hurt is thyne honesty,
Conciddering that no flour is so perfyt,
So full of vertew, plesans, and delyt,
So full of blisfull angellik bewty,
Imperiall birth, honour and dignite.'

Than to the Ros scho turnyt hir visage
And said, 'O lusty dochtir most benyng,
Aboif the lilly illustare of lynnage,
Fro the stok ryell rysing fresche and ying,
But ony spot or macull doing spring;
Cum, blowme of joy, with jemis to be cround,
For our the laif thy bewty is renownd.'

A coistly croun with clarefeid stonis brycht
This cumly quene did on hir heid inclois,
Quhill all the land illumynit of the licht:
Quhairfoir me thocht all flouris did rejos,
Crying attonis, 'Haill be thow richest Ros,
Haill hairbis empryce, haill freschest quene of flouris;
To the be glory and honour at all houris.'

Thane all the birdis song with voce on hicht,
Quhois mirthfull soun wes mervelus to heir:
The mavys song, 'Haill Rois most riche and richt,
That dois up flureis undir Phebus speir;
Haill plant of yowth, haill princes dochtir deir,
Haill blosome breking out of the blud royall,
Quhois pretius vertew is imperiall.'

The merle scho sang, 'Haill Rois of most delyt,
Haill of all flouris quene and soverane';
The lark scho song, 'Haill Rois both reid and quhyt,
Most plesand flour of michty cullouris twane';
The nychtingaill song, 'Haill Naturis suffragene
In bewty, nurtour, and every nobilnes,
In riche array, renown, and gentilnes.'

The commoun voce uprais of birdis small
Apone this wys, 'O blissit be the hour
That thow wes chosin to be our principall;
Welcome to be our princes of honour,
Our perle, our plesans and our paramour,
Our peax, our play, our plane felicite:
Chryst the conserf frome all adversite.'

Than all the birdis song with sic a schout
That I annone awoilk quhair that I lay,
And with a braid I turnyt me about

To se this court, bot all wer went away:
Than up I lenyt, halflingis in affrey,
And thus I wret, as ye haif hard to forrow,
Off lusty May upone the nynt morrow.

In back of the real

railroad yard in San Jose
        I wandered desolate
in front of a tank factory
        and sat on a bench
near the switchman's shack.

A flower lay on the hay on
        the asphalt highway
– the dread hay flower
        I thought – It had a
brittle black stem and
        corolla of yellowish dirty
spikes like Jesus' inchlong
        crown, and a soiled
dry center cotton tuft
        like a used shaving brush
that's been lying under
        the garage for a year.

Yellow, yellow flower, and
        flower of industry,
tough spikey ugly flower,
        flower nonetheless,
with the form of the great yellow
        Rose in your brain!
This is the flower of the World.

God's Grandeur

The world is charged with the grandeur of God.
    It will flame out, like shining from shook foil;
    It gathers to a greatness, like the ooze of oil
Crushed. Why do men then now not reck his rod?
Generations have trod, have trod, have trod;
    And all is seared with trade; bleared, smeared with toil;
    And wears man's smudge and shares man's smell: the soil
Is bare now, nor can foot feel, being shod.

And for all this, nature is never spent;
    There lives the dearest freshness deep down things;
And though the last lights off the black West went
    Oh, morning, at the brown brink eastward, springs –
Because the Holy Ghost over the bent
    World broods with warm breast and with ah! bright wings.

Ballad of the Clairvoyant Widow

A kindly Widow Lady, who lived upon a hill,
Climbed to her attic window and gazed across the sill.

'Oh tell me, Widow Lady, what is it that you see,
As you look across my city, in God's country?'

'I see ten million windows, I see ten thousand streets,
I see the traffic doing miraculous feats.

The lawyers all are cunning, the business men are fat,
Their wives go out on Sunday beneath the latest hat.

The kids play cops and robbers, the kids play mumbley-peg,
Some learn the art of thieving, and some grow up to beg;

The rich can play at polo, the poor can do the shag,
Professors are condoning the cultural lag.

I see a banker's mansion with twenty wood-grate fires,
Alone, his wife is grieving for what her heart desires.

Next door there is a love-nest of plaster board and tin,
The rats soon will be leaving, the snow will come in.'

'Clairvoyant Widow Lady, with an eye like a telescope,
Do you see any sign or semblance of that thing called "Hope"?'

'I see the river harbor, alive with men and ships,
A surgeon guides a scalpel with thumb and finger-tips.

I see grandpa surviving a series of seven strokes,
The unemployed are telling stale unemployment jokes.

The gulls ride on the water, the gulls have come and gone,
The men on rail and roadway keep moving on and on.

The salmon climb the rivers, the rivers nudge the sea,
The green comes up forever in the fields of our country.'

from Leaves of Grass: 15

The pure contralto sings in the organloft,
The carpenter dresses his plank. . . . the tongue of his foreplane
    whistles its wild ascending lisp,
The married and unmarried children ride home to their thanks-
    giving dinner,
The pilot seizes the king-pin, he heaves down with a strong arm,
The mate stands braced in the whaleboat, lance and harpoon are
    ready,
The duck-shooter walks by silent and cautious stretches,
The deacons are ordained with crossed hands at the altar,
The spinning-girl retreats and advances to the hum of the big wheel,
The farmer stops by the bars of a Sunday and looks at the oats
    and rye,
The lunatic is carried at last to the asylum a confirmed case,
He will never sleep any more as he did in the cot in his mother's
    bedroom;
The jour printer with gray head and gaunt jaws works at his case,
He turns his quid of tobacco, his eyes get blurred with the
    manuscript;
The malformed limbs are tied to the anatomist's table,
What is removed drops horribly in a pail:
The quadroon girl is sold at the stand . . . the drunkard nods by
    the barroom stove,
The machinist rolls up his sleeves . . . the policeman travels his
    beat . . . the gatekeeper marks who pass,
The young fellow drives the express-wagon . . . I love him though
    I do not know him;
The half-breed straps on his light boots to compete in the race,
The western turkey-shooting draws old and young . . . some lean
    on their rifles, some sit on logs,

Out from the crowd steps the marksman and takes his position and levels his piece;

The groups of newly-come immigrants cover the wharf or levee,

The woollypates hoe in the sugarfield, the overseer views them from his saddle;

The bugle calls in the ballroom, the gentlemen run for their partners, the dancers bow to each other;

The youth lies awake in the cedar-roofed garret and harks to the musical rain,

The Wolverine sets traps on the creek that helps fill the Huron,

The reformer ascends the platform, he spouts with his mouth and nose,

The company returns from its excursion, the darkey brings up the rear and bears the well-riddled target,

The squaw wrapt in her yellow-hemmed cloth is offering moccasins and beadbags for sale,

The connoisseur peers along the exhibition-gallery with halfshut eyes bent sideways,

The deckhands make fast the steamboat, the plank is thrown for the shoregoing passengers,

The young sister holds out the skein, the elder sister winds it off in a ball and stops now and then for the knots,

The one-year wife is recovering and happy, a week ago she bore her first child,

The cleanhaired Yankee girl works with her sewing-machine or in the factory or mill,

The nine months' gone is in the parturition chamber, her faintness and pains are advancing;

The pavingman leans on his twohanded rammer – the reporter's lead flies swiftly over the notebook – the signpainter is lettering with red and gold,

The canal-boy trots on the towpath – the bookkeeper counts at his desk – the shoemaker waxes his thread,

The conductor beats time for the band and all the performers
follow him,
The child is baptised – the convert is making the first professions,
The regatta is spread on the bay . . . how the white sails sparkle!
The drover watches his drove, he sings out to them that would
stray,
The pedlar sweats with his pack on his back – the purchaser
higgles about the odd cent,
The camera and plate are prepared, the lady must sit for her
daguerreotype,
The bride unrumples her white dress, the minutehand of the
clock moves slowly,
The opium eater reclines with rigid head and just-opened lips,
The prostitute draggles her shawl, her bonnet bobs on her tipsy
and pimpled neck,
The crowd laugh at her blackguard oaths, the men jeer and wink
to each other,
(Miserable! I do not laugh at your oaths nor jeer you,)
The President holds a cabinet council, he is surrounded by the
great secretaries,
On the piazza walk five friendly matrons with twined arms;
The crew of the fish-smack pack repeated layers of halibut in the
hold,
The Missourian crosses the plains toting his wares and his cattle,
The fare-collector goes through the train – he gives notice by the
jingling of loose change,
The floormen are laying the floor – the tinners are tinning the
roof – the masons are calling for mortar,
In single file each shouldering his hod pass onward the laborers;
Seasons pursuing each other the indescribable crowd is gathered . . .
it is the Fourth of July . . . what salutes of cannon and small arms!
Seasons pursuing each other the plougher ploughs and the mower
mows and the wintergrain falls in the ground;

Off on the lakes the pikefisher watches and waits by the hole in the frozen surface,

The stumps stand thick round the clearing, the squatter strikes deep with his axe,

The flatboatmen make fast toward dusk near the cottonwood or pekantrees,

The coon-seekers go now through the regions of the Red river, or through those drained by the Tennessee, or through those of the Arkansas,

The torches shine in the dark that hangs on the Chattahoochee or Altamahaw;

Patriarchs sit at supper with sons and grandsons and great grandsons around them,

In walls of adobie, in canvas tents, rest hunters and trappers after their day's sport.

The city sleeps and the country sleeps,

The living sleep for their time . . . the dead sleep for their time,

The old husband sleeps by his wife and the young husband sleeps by his wife;

And these one and all tend inward to me, and I tend outward to them,

And such as it is to be of these more or less I am.

Pastures of Plenty

It's a mighty hard road that my poor hands have hoed,
My poor feet have travelled a hot dusty road,
Out of your dust bowl and westward we roll,
Through deserts so hot and your mountains so cold.

I've wandered all over your green growing land,
Wherever your crops are I've lent you my hand,
On the edge of your cities you'll see me and then,
I come with the dust and I'm gone with the wind.

California, Arizona, I've worked on your crops,
Then north up to Oregon to gather your hops,
Dig beets from your ground, I cut grapes from your vines,
To set on your tables that light sparklin' wine.

Green Pastures of plenty from dry desert ground,
From the Grand Coulee dam where the water runs down,
Ev'ry State of this Union us migrants have been,
We come with the dust and we're gone with the wind.

It's always we ramble that river and I,
All along your green valleys I'll work till I die,
I'll travel this road until death sets me free,
'Cause my Pastures of plenty must always be free.

It's a mighty hard road that my poor hands have hoed,
My poor feet have travelled this hot dusty road,
On the edge of your cities you'll see me and then,
I come with the dust and I'm gone with the wind.

WOODY GUTHRIE

An Epitaph at Great Torrington, Devon

Here lies a man who was killed by lightning;
He died when his prospects seemed to be brightening.
He might have cut a flash in this world of trouble,
But the flash cut him, and he lies in the stubble.

'Erthë tok of erthe'

Erthë tok of erthe
   erthë wyth wogh;
Erthe other erthë
   to the erthë drogh;

Erthë leyde erthe
   in erthënë throgh;
Tho hevëde erthe of erthe
   erthe ynogh.

Bog Queen

I lay waiting
between turf-face and demense wall,
between heathery levels
and glass-toothed stone.

My body was braille
for the creeping influences:
dawn suns groped over my head
and cooled at my feet,

through my fabrics and skins
the seeps of winter
digested me,
the illiterate roots

pondered and died
in the cavings
of stomach and socket.
I lay waiting

on the gravel bottom,
my brain darkening,
a jar of spawn
fermenting underground

dreams of Baltic amber.
Bruised berries under my nails,
the vital hoard reducing
in the crock of the pelvis.

My diadem grew carious,
gemstones dropped

in the peat floe
like the bearings of history.

My sash was a black glacier
wrinkling, dyed weaves
and phoenician stitchwork
retted on my breasts'

soft moraines.
I knew winter cold
like the nuzzle of fjords
at my thighs –

the soaked fledge, the heavy
swaddle of hides.
My skull hibernated
in the wet nest of my hair.

Which they robbed.
I was barbered
and stripped
by a turfcutter's spade

who veiled me again
and packed coomb softly
between the stone jambs
at my head and my feet.

that has tanned and toughened.
The cured wound
opens inwards to a dark
elderberry place.

Who will say 'corpse'
to his vivid cast?
Who will say 'body'
to his opaque repose?

And his rusted hair,
a mat unlikely
as a foetus's.
I first saw his twisted face

in a photograph,
a head and shoulder
out of the peat,
bruised like a forceps baby,

but now he lies
perfected in my memory,
down to the red horn
of his nails,

hung in the scales
with beauty and atrocity:
with the Dying Gaul
too strictly compassed

on his shield,
with the actual weight
of each hooded victim,
slashed and dumped.

The River God

Of the River Mimram in Hertfordshire

I may be smelly and I may be old,
Rough in my pebbles, reedy in my pools,
But where my fish float by I bless their swimming
And I like the people to bathe in me, especially women.
But I can drown the fools
Who bathe too close to the weir, contrary to rules.
And they take a long time drowning
As I throw them up now and then in a spirit of clowning.
Hi yih, yippity-yap, merrily I flow,
O I may be an old foul river but I have plenty of go.
Once there was a lady who was too bold
She bathed in me by the tall black cliff where the water runs cold,
So I brought her down here
To be my beautiful dear.
Oh will she stay with me will she stay
This beautiful lady, or will she go away?
She lies in my beautiful deep river bed with many a weed
To hold her, and many a waving reed.
Oh who would guess what a beautiful white face lies there
Waiting for me to smoothe and wash away the fear
She looks at me with. Hi yih, do not let her
Go. There is no one on earth who does not forget her
Now. They say I am a foolish old smelly river
But they do not know of my wide original bed
Where the lady waits, with her golden sleepy head.
If she wishes to go I will not forgive her.

Heat Wave

After it rained, the back roads gusted with steam,
and the gardens along our street filled with the scent
of stocks and nicotiana,
but it didn't get properly hot till the night drew in,
humid and heavy as glass
on our well-kept lawn.
It was high in the summer. With everyone else
in town for the Lammas fair
I took the meadow-path to where the river
stalled on a sudden blackness: alders
shrouded in night and warmth, and the first slow owl
charting the further bank.

There was always movement there
beneath the slick of moonlight on the turning
water, like a life beneath the life
I understood as cattle tracks and birds:
a darker presence, rising from the stream,
to match my every move, my every breath.
Eel-black and cold, it melded in my flesh
with all the nooks and crannies of the world
where spawn appears, or changelings slip their skins
to ripen at the damp edge of the day,
still blurred with mud
and unrecovered song.

But that night, as the sky above me turned,
I found a different swimmer in the steady
shimmer of the tide,
a living creature, come from the other side
to slip into the cool

black water. I remember how she looked,
beneath the moon, so motiveless and white,
her body like a pod that had been shelled
and emptied: Mrs Pearce, my younger sister's
science teacher, turning in the lit
amazement of a joy that I could almost
smell, across the haze of drifting heat.

I was crouched beneath a stand
of willows and I guess she didn't see
the boy who watched her swim for half an hour
then turn for home beneath the August moon,
a half-smile on her face, her auburn hair
straggling and damp;
yet later, as I walked the usual streets,
I thought that she would stop and recognise
a fellow soul, with river in his eyes,
slipping home under a wave of light and noise,
and finding the key to her nights
in his soft, webbed fingers.

Under the Waterfall

'Whenever I plunge my arm, like this,
In a basin of water, I never miss
The sweet sharp sense of a fugitive day
Fetched back from its thickening shroud of gray.
    Hence the only prime
    And real love-rhyme
    That I know by heart,
    And that leaves no smart,
Is the purl of a little valley fall
About three spans wide and two spans tall
Over a table of solid rock,
And into a scoop of the self-same block;
The purl of a runlet that never ceases
In stir of kingdoms, in wars, in peaces;
With a hollow boiling voice it speaks
And has spoken since hills were turfless peaks.'

'And why gives this the only prime
Idea to you of a real love-rhyme?
And why does plunging your arm in a bowl
Full of spring water, bring throbs to your soul?'

'Well, under the fall, in a crease of the stone,
Though where precisely none ever has known,
Jammed darkly, nothing to show how prized,
And by now with its smoothness opalized,
    Is a drinking-glass:
    For, down that pass
    My lover and I
    Walked under a sky

THOMAS HARDY

Of blue with a leaf-wove awning of green,
In the burn of August, to paint the scene,
And we placed our basket of fruit and wine
By the runlet's rim, where we sat to dine;
And when we had drunk from the glass together,
Arched by the oak-copse from the weather,
I held the vessel to rinse in the fall,
Where it slipped, and sank, and was past recall,
Though we stooped and plumbed the little abyss
With long bared arms. There the glass still is.
And, as said, if I thrust my arm below
Cold water in basin or bowl, a throe
From the past awakens a sense of that time,
And the glass we used, and the cascade's rhyme.
The basin seems the pool, and its edge
The hard smooth face of the brook-side ledge,
And the leafy pattern of china-ware
The hanging plants that were bathing there.

'By night, by day, when it shines or lours,
There lies intact that chalice of ours,
And its presence adds to the rhyme of love
Persistently sung by the fall above.
No lip has touched it since his and mine
In turns therefrom sipped lovers' wine.'

The Lost Parasol

I think there is much more in even the smallest creation of God,
should it only be an ant, than wise men think.
St Teresa of Avila

Where metalled road invades light thinning air,
some twenty steps more and a steep gorge yawns
with its jagged crest, and the sky is rounder there,
    it is like the world's end;
nearer: bushy glade in flower,
farther: space, rough mountain folk;
    a young man called his lover
    to go up in the cool of daybreak,
they took their rest in the grass, they lay down;
the girl has left her red parasol behind.

Wood shades sunshade. Quietness all round.
What can be there, with no one to be seen?
Time pours out its measureless froth and
    the near and the far still unopened
    and midday comes and evening comes,
no midday there, no evening, eternal floods
that swim in the wind, the fog, the light, the world
and this tangle moves off into endlessness
like a gigantic shimmering silk cocoon,
skirted by wells of flame and craters of soot.

Dawn, a pearl-grey ferry, was drifting
    on its bright herd of clouds,
from the valley the first cow-bell came ringing
and the couple walked forward, head by head;
    now their souvenir clings to the shadows,
    red silk, the leaves, the green light on it, filtering,

SÁNDOR WEÖRES   [106

metal frame, bone handle, button:
   separate thing from the order of men,
   it came home intact, the parasol,
its neighbours rockface and breeze, its land cold soil.

In a sun-rocked cradle which is as massive
   as the very first creation itself
      the little one lies, light instrument
   on the blue-grey mossy timber of a cliff,
   around it the stray whistling, the eternal murmuring
   of the forest, vast Turkey-oak, slim hornbeam,
   briar-thickets, a thousand sloe-bushes quivering,
   noble tranquil ranks of created things,
   and among them only the parasol flares out:
jaunty far-off visitor whose clothes still shout.

Languidly, as if long established there,
   its new home clasps it about:
   the rocks hug their squat stonecrops,
   above it the curly heliotropes
      cat's-tail veronica,
   wild pinks push through cage of thistles,
   dragon-fly broods on secret convolvulus,
   dries his gauze wings, totters out:
   so life goes on here, never otherwise –
a chink in the leaves, a flash of blue-smiling skies.

The huge-lunged forest breathes at it
   like yesterday, like long ago,
   mild smell of the soft nest of a girl.
      Shy green woodpecker and russet
   frisky squirrel refused to sit on it,
   who knows what it hides: man left it;
   but a nosy hedgehog comes up to the ledge,

the prickly loafer, low of leg,
   like a steam puffer patrols round the rock;
puts heart in the woodpecker tapping at his trunk.

The sun stretches out its muscular rays:
   you would expect the bell of heaven to crack.
   Broad world – so many small worlds find their place
   in you! Through the closed parasol's hills and valleys
   an oblong speck moves: an ant that drags
   the headless abdomen of a locust with rapt
   persistence and effort: up to the bare heights,
   down to the folds, holding the load tight,
   and turning back at the very end of the way,
floundering up again with the body. Who knows why?

This finger-long journey is not shorter or sillier
   than Everything, and its aim is just as hidden.
   Look: through the branches you can see the hillside,
   there a falcon, a spot on the clear sky,
   hangs in the air like a bird of stone:
   predator, hanging over from history.
   Here, wolf and brown bear were once at home,
   crystalline lynx lay in ambush for the innocent.
   God wetted a finger, turned a page
and the world had a very different image.

A sky-splitting single-sloped precipice,
   its lap a lemon-yellow corrie of sand,
   far off a rosy panorama of mist,
   curly hills in a ragged mauve cloud-band;
   above, the couple stood; below, the sun-wheel stirred;
   in the dawn-flames, so interdependent
   they stood, afraid, at the very edge of fate;
   boulders rolled from beneath their feet,

they were quarrelling, tearing their hearts,
each of them deaf before the other starts.

In the tangled thicket of their young blood
the luminous world skulks off, sinks;
    shame like a rose-branch cut
        the boy to the quick:
beyond entreaty, ready to throw himself down to . . .
His white shirt gestured against the blue,
    at the shrubby scarp with its bindweed
        he lurched forward, forward
growing smaller and more distant – and his frightened girl
runs after him through briars, her knee's blood is a pearl.

Tall sedges lean over the gorge
and like a gemmed porch of the depths below
an army of tiny shining shields of weeds
    and a thick dark couch of green
cling round the bark of a stump that points no-
where, here their frenzy lost its rage:
they twined together, to ask why, to cry,
like the horned moon the white flash of a thigh;
a hooded boletus at their feet
fattened its spore-crammed belly, not bothering to mate.

    The hilltop sends down
        wind tasting of stone
    to crochet sudden air-lace;
    and the lost parasol
    shivers and half lives;
in the endlessly intricate forest, in the deep maze
    of its undergrowth, a breeze
lurks, but takes off at the sharp rock-fall,
    pouring over that solitary wall
and across the ravine, flying light to the dale.

Zigzag mane of the thicket
          wavers and swirls,
     the forest depths are sighing,
a thousand tiny leaves, like birds' tails, flicker
     and glint in the light like scales;
drawn up from a breeze-wakened copse
yeasty, spicy fragrances are flying;
     a snapped thorn-branch stirs, drops,
          catches on the soft fabric:
on the tent-like parasol the first tear is pricked.

     No one is sorry –
right above it an oriole is calling,
     inside it a bow-legged spider scurries
     round and round the scarlet corrie
and makes off: under the metal-arched ribs
a lizard twists in search of his siesta,
     he guzzles the oven-heat and like a jester
propped on both hands peeps out from the midst;
later some mice come running in and out
and the shaft has a gaudy tit perking about.

In the vault of summer skies, diamond-blue,
an ice-white lace-mist moves in a smile;
over the plain, at the foothills of heaven,
there are dark woolpacks hanging heavy
and truant cloud-lines in crumbling style;
Apollo, body stripped, striding through,
     runs young, strong, and fresh,
hot oil steams on the earth's rough flesh;
in air that rocks both valley and peak,
in empty immensities – a red spot of silk.

The girl of the neglected parasol
is just as small, lost in the broad world,

a tiny insect dropped in a sea-wide flood;
    no one to talk to at all,
wrapping her own soul round her fear,
   she curls up in a curtained room,
   and hears a whipped dog whining there
   as if there was no misery anywhere,
no other wound to ache in earth or heaven;
or does he howl for all the pain of men?

      Hanging on the sky's arch
        at the lower bank
          the dusk
          is hazy.
   The first? How many before? On the lazy
   ridge no grass or insect measures it,
   neither cuckoo nor cuckoo-spit,
the twilights turn for ever, as created.
At the rock's edge, with forever's speed
the sleek silk vanishes into foaming shade.

Night's victory, yesterday's goodbye:
huge galley in the bay of earth and sky,
floating catafalque of dead Osiris;
scarlet embers fall into saffron high-tide,
peacock of air bends his fan from the heights,
shimmering feathers are roses and night-stocks;
an organ of gold installed in space
opens up all its pipes and lips,
pencils of light-rays spring from the rifts
and stroke the hills while darkness fills their cliffs.

      On the foamy crest of foliage
   light and shade come knotted together
   like the body's pain and pleasure.

Fading now, from its cover, the cuckoo's message,
        and the motley unison
of piping, chattering, chirping, splashing
        prankishness and passion.
    The evening light, that turns dreams on,
    bends through the cool slow-surging trees,
gleams in the silvery homespun of twittering beaks.

        Each smallest voice is poured
        delicately into the quiet;
    the nightingale among thorns, like
        a plucked metal string
    casts a few notes into the wind,
    then uncoils one ringing thread
        floating and spinning,
    then flicks it like a veil, languid,
    then bunches it rippling, potent but light,
and it fades: into a bed carved out of quiet.

    The western sky is drained
    of the late dusk's arching marble veins
    and the lit-up, burnt-out body of the sky
        leaves a steep column of smoke,
    pierced through by stars as sharp as steel:
    pearl-crest of Boötes between waving trees,
    Cygnus a cross drifting lazily by,
    Cassiopeia with its double dagger, the rope
    of the faintly glimmering Milky Way
loosely folding dead black space away.

    The valley, a deep arena, rests,
    crisscrossed by shadows of slashed buttresses;
        in the cirque a buxom Venus dances,
    approaches, spins round, offers riches,

dances naked, white as snow, touches
her feet upon the dew-drenched hills,
soft-bodied, plump, with shining curls,
the slippery form is merged in darkness,
avid monsters stare her through and through;
in a swoon she waves goodbye and the curtain snaps to.

Like rows of houses in an earthquake:
great tangle of trees at the wood's edge
   stagger and shake;
a green shot flies up into the whirlwind,
a grindstone shrieking comes from rocky ledge,
the wilderness tosses and groans;
on the cloud-capped hilltop a thin
lightning burns, crackles, cracks,
then the long crisped fires streaming like flax
split above the cliff, a lion's growl at their backs.

The storm flickers through the twigs,
its thousand necks turn and twist,
it wrestles with the stumbling forest,
a writhing timber in its fist,
leathery roots clutch hard,
lightning tingles in the dark,
hundreds of birds crouch and start
in nests that shake them to the heart,
the burning, clammy monster rages still,
the sky, bowed low, seethes around the hill.

Torn-off leaves whirl anywhere,
roots of a gouged beech prod the air;
the parasol has been swept off the rock,
into a bramble-bush, beside a tree-trunk,
the downpour slaps its silk,

it is all smudged now, frayed, and the ribs show.
   It is indifferent to its fate – as the hilltop holds
   its head without complaint in thunderbolts,
      and with the sky huddles low,
and fixed by sticky clouds watches the daybreak glow.

     The parasol has a new home:
the secret world in fallen leaves,
cool dark earth and mouldering grove,
pallid trailers, roots in graves,
horrors endless, puffy, ropy, cold,
   centipede country, maggot metropolis;
   the days swing round like catapults,
casting the full sun over it, the old
weltering moon; and the parasol sprawls
like a flaking corpse, though it never lived at all.

Autumn rustles: stuffs dead leaves in it;
   winter gallops: it is all snow;
   the thaw sets it free again:
      earth-brown, washed-out now.
   A sprouting acorn pushes,
      and through the slack, loose
      fabric a tiny flag
      thrusts the fibres back:
green, tender tassel steers to the weathervanes;
a few more years and a tree will shade the remains.

The parasol has changed: it has left human hands;
the girl has changed too: she is the woman of a man;
once, the red sail and the steerer ran
   lightly together, roving free,
while hosts of drunkenly foaming plum trees
tempted the wasps to stir noisily

and deep in the girl's heart the bumble-bees
   began to swarm and buzz mischievously;
   since then, this wild army has been busy,
building a fortress in her woman's body.

   Both man and woman have forgotten it now,
   though it was the first witness of their linked fates:
   Lombard silk and red Rhine dye,
   long-travelled Indian ivory,
   Pittsburgh iron, Brazilian wood, how
      many handcarts have trundled its parts,
      they have gone by rail, they have gone in boats:
   a world to make it! son of a thousand hands!
   yet no curio: old-world frippery;
lost: no joy in that, yet no great misery.

   Branching veins draw it into the dark,
      light-unvisited mud weighs it down,
   it is mere rags, dying in dribs and drabs,
   it has stopped serving exotic demands
   and like a bird escaping its cage-door
      takes up its great home:
   the dissolving soil, the swirl of space, the rays
   draw it all ways, confused, astray,
   old shoreless floods map its new phase:
this is creation's first emergent day.

   Neither sun, moon, nor watch
      can measure creation's second and third days:
      the father of vegetation keeps his watch
   over it, clod-head, Saturn, dark face
   with grey eyebrows hanging to his chin.
      Pulsing life-fluid filters in:
   powdered cloth, rotten wood, rusted iron

dissolve and disappear in tangle and thorn,
and slowly sucked by each capillary vein
it seethes alive again in the humming vortex of green.

Its handle is visible through the leaf-mould.
A brown moth settles there, perches awhile.
      By midnight it has laid
hundreds of eggs, a mass of tiny balls
placed in smooth strips, finely embroidered.
And like a biblical ancestress
she opens her wings, floats victorious,
queen fulfilled in happiness,
      not caring that dawn brings death:
God in the sky drew up my trembling crest!

The parasol no longer exists: bit by bit
      it set off into the open world,
      all changed, part after part;
even the eyes of Argus might find no trace,
         swivelling across the light,
         sliding down to the shade;
      only a single feeble fibre remains,
      poised on the top of a bramble-prickle,
      it is mere fluff, next to invisible;
flies up from the thorn-prick, jumps into the saddle

of a storm! Lily-thin air-pockets toss it on,
      the mountains shift below
in stampede, buffalo trampling buffalo;
fog-blanket opens on dark forest paths,
brooks twinkling down in the shy straths,
sharp drop of the crag wall, a mine,
toy trains of tubs moving along the rails,
scattered homesteads, a town with its smoke-trails,

and overhead, the great bleak acres of silence
and below, the hill from which the tuft went flying.

Upwards, still higher up it floats:
the moon hangs close like a white fruit,
the earth is a round, tilted, blotchy shroud
    framed by blackness and void.
        Bathed in airy juices,
the fluff swings heavy like a full leather bottle,
    descends to the ground, settles:
    on a green plain, in drizzly mists,
it hovers lightly among the acacias
and probes a calf's ear as its resting-place.

A thunderstorm crashes, carries it off,
flies with it raggedly over moor and bog,
like a spool it turns, winding the fog,
    and when it is all spun onto a distaff:
low blue sea and high blue sky are combers,
    two sun discs gaze at each other
    and between the two blue shells
        a tiny sail
        sways, tranquil,
uncaring whether it sways in air or swell.

The vapour-tulip throws back its head,
a glass-green other-worldly meadow glistens,
at the horizon a purple thorn gathers;
darkness surrounds the far-off island;
a little ray like a woman's glance flickers,
vanishes caressing the lover, glitters
as it flutters onto its drowsy son,
while a smile dawns eternity on man,
its arches bend and march on their way
between watery shores, Theatrum Gloriae Dei.

*   *   *

The red silk parasol was my song,
　　sung for my only one;
this true love is the clearest spring,
　　I have smoothed its mirror with my breath,
I have seen the two of us, the secret is known:
　　we shall moulder into one after death.
Now I expend my life exultantly
like the oriole in the tree:
till it falls down on the old forest floor,
singing with such full throat its heart must burst and soar.

Translated from the Hungarian
by Edwin Morgan

Moss

Long ago the advance guard of vegetation came to a halt on the rocks, which were dumbfounded. A thousand silken velvet rods then sat down cross-legged.

From then on, ever since moss with its lance-bearers started twitching on bare rock, all nature has been caught in an inextricable predicament and, trapped underneath, panics, stampedes, suffocates.

Worse yet, hairs grew; with time, everything got darker.

Oh obsession with longer and longer hairs! Deep carpets that kneel when you sit on them now lift themselves in muddled aspiration. Hence not only suffocations but drownings.

Well, we could just scalp the old, severe, solid rock of these terry-cloth landscapes, these soggy doormats: it would be feasible, saturated as they are.

Translated from the French
by C. K. Williams

Thinking about Aboriginal Land Rights, I Visit the Farm I Will Not Inherit

Watching from the barn the seedlight and nearly-all-down
currents of a spring day, I see the only lines bearing
consistent strain are the straight ones: fence, house corner,
outermost furrows. The drifts of grass coming and canes
are whorled and sod-bunching, are issuant, with dusts.
The wind-lap outlines of lagoons are pollen-concurred
and the light rising out of them stretches in figments and wings.
The ambient day-tides contain every mouldering and oil
that the bush would need to come back right this day,
not suddenly, but all down the farm slopes, the polished shell
     barks
flaking, leaves noon-thin, with shale stones and orchids at foot
and the creek a hung gallery again, and the bee trees unrobbed.
By sundown it is dense dusk, all the tracks closing in.
I go into the earth near the feed shed for thousands of years.

Wodwo

What am I? Nosing here, turning leaves over
Following a faint stain on the air to the river's edge
I enter water. What am I to split
The glassy grain of water looking upward I see the bed
Of the river above me upside down very clear
What am I doing here in mid-air? Why do I find
this frog so interesting as I inspect its most secret
interior and make it my own? Do these weeds
know me and name me to each other have they
seen me before, do I fit in their world? I seem
separate from the ground and not rooted but dropped
out of nothing casually I've no threads
fastening me to anything I can go anywhere
I seem to have been given the freedom
of this place what am I then? And picking
bits of bark off this rotten stump gives me
no pleasure and it's no use so why do I do it
me and doing that have coincided very queerly
But what shall I be called am I the first
have I an owner what shape am I what
shape am I am I huge if I go
to the end on this way past these trees and past these trees
till I get tired that's touching one wall of me
for the moment if I sit still how everything
stops to watch me I suppose I am the exact centre
but there's all this what is it roots
roots roots roots and here's the water
again very queer but I'll go on looking

from From an Abandoned Work

Up bright and early that day, I was young then, feeling awful, and out, mother hanging out of the window in her nightdress weeping and waving. Nice fresh morning, bright too early as so often. Feeling really awful, very violent. The sky would soon darken and rain fall and go on falling, all day, till evening. Then blue and sun again a second, then night. Feeling all this, how violent and the kind of day, I stopped and turned. So back with bowed head on the look out for a snail, slug or worm. Great love in my heart too for all things still and rooted, bushes, boulders and the like, too numerous to mention, even the flowers of the field, not for the world when in my right senses would I ever touch one, to pluck it. Whereas a bird now, or a butterfly, fluttering about and getting in my way, all moving things, getting in my path, a slug now, getting under my feet, no, no mercy. Not that I'd go out of my way to get at them, no, at a distance often they seemed still, then a moment later they were upon me. Birds with my piercing sight I have seen flying so high, so far, that they seemed at rest, then the next minute they were all about me, crows have done this. Ducks are perhaps the worst, to be suddenly stamping and stumbling in the midst of ducks, or hens, any class of poultry, few things are worse. Nor will I go out of my way to avoid such things, when avoidable, no, I simply will not go out of my way, though I have never in my life been on my way anywhere, but simply on my way. And in this way I have gone through great thickets, bleeding, and deep into bogs, water too, even the sea in some moods and been carried out of my course, or driven back, so as not to drown. And that is perhaps how I shall die at last if they don't catch me, I mean drowned, or in fire, yes, perhaps that is how I shall do it at last, walking furious headlong into fire and dying burnt to bits.

SAMUEL BECKETT   [122

Trap Door

Last night went walking with a woman that I know
we went down to the marsh land
as I like to call those fresh plowed fields
just back of town
that after all once used to be a marsh
just as the skies on certain days are one big bog
& it was getting to be fall

So we had been out walking for an hour now
& it was just as wonderful as to forget
the world & then yourself
& just as wonderful forgetting you had ever lived
& I felt rotten like a drowned man they bring back to life
& when this lady friend just suddenly spoke up
I felt as rotten as a drowned man who already had forgotten he
    had ever lived

Lucky that her words had no fixed meaning
she just said
how sad I am
& then
how grim these streets are that end up as fields
& even more
I'm horrified by all those distant lights
those unsure graveyard lights those distant lights
& then
how sad to look into those windows where people sit & eat their
    evening meals

And I just stood there owing her an answer
the way a wet leaf owes it to a spark
the way a trumpet owes it to the evening

a mirror, blind from cobwebs, to a candle
wax when it stiffens to the ring that seals it in
I was still owing her an answer & we kept walking on without
    a word

Then it seemed to me
but only for an instant
as if the earth had been derailed & sinking down
& I was falling with the countryside & all
I kept on falling
while I still was walking on firm ground
I kept on falling & it made me feel real dizzy
but not with vertigo this time around
I kept on falling like a tower that sees its birds fly off
I kept on falling like a man his memory abandons
I kept on falling & was feeling no real pain
I kept on falling like a glowing cigar that burns down while still
    falling
I kept on falling like a paper on fire the poem on it disappearing
I kept on falling like the seat on a swing shaped like a boat
I kept on falling like a drop falling into the snow
like a bell falling into a lake
like a babe falling into a feather bed
like a nut falling onto a bolt
I kept on falling & not feeling the shock
& falling with the countryside in which an unseen bog is hidden
falling with the feeling of forgetting
& reality moved further off, would slowly fall to pieces
like the comb atop a rooster's head
like the pitch that flows out of a star before it dies
like a midnight fly at midnight
like a telegram there in the woods
like the smile of dew at high noon
I was falling like the earth in flight across the universe

Hail thy gliding flight, o Wing of Death
those who tried to brace themselves against it
all have purple faces
all have bloodshot eyes like drying grape leaves
ugly scars across their foreheads
nails that dig into the lines over your hand
hairs trembling standing end on end
a wooden tongue & limbs made out of stone

O may I die without resistance give myself to Death
the way a patient gives himself to anesthesia
the way a wounded man seeks out the surgeon's knife
the way exhausted eyes succumb to sleep
the way my hands surrender to my thoughts
that pass like ever changing clouds over the dislodged earth

Translated from the Czech
by Jerome Rothenberg and Milos Sovak

Secret Road

Its name is secret road, the one which few people know, which not all people are aware of, which few people go along. It is good, fine; a good place, a fine place. It is where one is harmed, a place of harm. It is known as a safe place; it is a difficult place, a dangerous place. One is frightened. It is a place of fear.

There are trees, crags, gorges, rivers, precipitous places, places of precipitous land, various places of precipitous land, various precipitous places, gorges, various gorges. It is a place of wild animals, a place of wild beasts, full of wild beasts. It is a place where one is put to death by stealth; a place where one is put to death in the jaws of the wild beasts of the land of the dead.

I take the secret road. I follow along, I encounter the secret road. He goes following along, he goes joining that which is bad, the corner, the darkness, the secret road. He goes to seek, to find, that which is bad.

Translated from the Aztec Dictionary
compiled by Bernadino de Sahagún,
translated by Charles E. Dibble and Arthur J. O. Anderson

ANONYMOUS

Naming the Field

We here call this *grass*, you can pick it
like this, it is the earth's *hair*, feel *hair*
on your head. Pick a *strand*
of *grass*, one of the earth's *hairs*,
you can whistle through it like this,
you can chew it and, spread out,
it is a kind of *carpet*. This is what we call *rock*
sticking through the *carpet*, the *rock* is not a *strand*
but is *hard*, like my *head*, you see, if I tap it,
but *harder* than *head*. This, flowing through the *field*,
we call *stream*. *Field* is *carpet* between *hedges*
and *stream* divides it. Is this place the end

of your pilgrimage or are you passing only,
have you become astray here? *Hedge*
is what we call this *flowing* upwards of *shrubs* and *bushes*,
of *runners* and *nests*, of parasitic *blooms*. The *field*
in its *flowing* to us through *time*

is named Saint Alphege's, who was beaten to death
with ox *bones*. These, under the skin, we call *bones*,
you see I am thin, my *bones* stick through almost
like *rocks*. This all around us, invisible
we call *air*, see when I *breathe* my *lungs*
fill with *air*. I have had my place here, I wash my *bones*
under my *skin*
in the *stream*, so as to be *clean*
when the *earth* claims me back. This – *splash, splash* –
we call *marsh*. These *reeds* in the *marsh*
are the long thin grave stones
of those who went straight *down*

thrilling to the call of the steep deep,
their *bodies* long thin needles – 'This won't hurt,
this won't hurt a bit.' I cannot explain *home*,
it is not *room*, nor is it contained within *stone* walls. The *stream*

is at *home* in *field, rocks* are,
air is, *grass* is, *honeysuckle* is – smell it
and *I* am.

from Reynard the Fox

From the Gallows Hill to the Tineton Copse
There were ten ploughed fields, like ten full-stops,
All wet red clay, where a horse's foot
Would be swathed, feet thick, like an ash-tree root.
The fox raced on, on the headlands firm,
Where his swift feet scared the coupling worm;
The rooks rose raving to curse him raw,
He snarled a sneer at their swoop and caw.
Then on, then on, down a half-ploughed field
Where a ship-like plough drove glitter-keeled,
With a bay horse near and a white horse leading,
And a man saying 'Zook,' and the red earth bleeding.
He gasped as he saw the ploughman drop
The stilts and swear at the team to stop.
The ploughman ran in his red clay clogs,
Crying, 'Zick un, Towzer; zick, good dogs!'
A couple of wire-haired lurchers lean
Arose from his wallet, nosing keen;
With a rushing swoop they were on his track,
Putting chest to stubble to bite his back.
He swerved from his line with the curs at heel,
The teeth as they missed him clicked like steel.
With a worrying snarl, they quartered on him,
While the ploughman shouted, 'Zick; upon him.'

The fox raced on, up the Barton Balks,
With a crackle of kex in the nettle stalks,
Over Hammond's grass to the dark green line
Of the larch-wood smelling of turpentine.
Scratch Steven Larches, black to the sky,
A sadness breathing with one long sigh,

Grey ghosts of trees under funeral plumes,
A mist of twig over soft brown glooms.
As he entered the wood he heard the smacks,
Chip-jar, of the fir-pole feller's axe.
He swerved to the left to a broad green ride,
Where a boy made him rush for the farther side.
He swerved to the left, to the Barton Road,
But there were the timberers come to load –
Two timber-carts and a couple of carters
With straps round their knees instead of garters.
He swerved to the right, straight down the wood,
The carters watched him, the boy hallooed.
He leaped from the larch-wood into tillage,
The cobbler's garden of Barton village.

The cobbler bent at his wooden foot,
Beating sprigs in a broken boot;
He wore old glasses with thick horn rim,
He scowled at his work, for his sight was dim.
His face was dingy, his lips were grey,
From primming sparrowbills day by day.
As he turned his boot he heard a noise
At his garden-end, and he thought, 'It's boys.'

Like a rocket shot to a ship ashore
The lean red bolt of his body tore,
Like a ripple of wind running swift on grass;
Like a shadow on wheat when a cloud blows past,
Like a turn at the buoy in a cutter sailing
When the bright green gleam lips white at the railing,
Like the April snake whipping back to sheath,
Like the gannets' hurtle on fish beneath,
Like a kestrel chasing, like a sickle reaping,
Like all things swooping, like all things sweeping,

Like a hound for stay, like a stag for swift,
With his shadow beside like spinning drift.

Past the gibbet-stock all stuck with nails,
Where they hanged in chains what had hung at jails,
Past Ashmundshowe where Ashmund sleeps,
And none but the tumbling peewit weeps,
Past Curlew Calling, the gaunt grey corner
Where the curlew comes as a summer mourner,
Past Blowbury Beacon, shaking his fleece,
Where all winds hurry and none brings peace;
Then down on the mile-long green decline,
Where the turf's like spring and the air's like wine,
Where the sweeping spurs of the downland spill
Into Wan Brook Valley and Wan Dyke Hill.

On he went with a galloping rally
Past Maesbury Clump for Wan Brook Valley.
The blood in his veins went romping high,
'Get on, on, on, to the earth or die.'
The air of the downs went purely past
Till he felt the glory of going fast,
Till the terror of death, though there indeed,
Was lulled for a while by his pride of speed.
He was romping away from hounds and hunt,
He had Wan Dyke Hill and his earth in front,
In a one mile more when his point was made
He would rest in safety from dog or spade;
Nose between paws he would hear the shout
Of the 'Gone to earth!' to the hounds without,
The whine of the hounds, and their cat-feet gadding
Scratching the earth, and their breath padpadding;
He would hear the horn call hounds away,
And rest in peace till another day.

from The Praise of Ben Dorain

Over mountains, pride
Of place to Ben Dorain!
I've nowhere espied
A finer to reign.
In her moorbacks wide
Hosts of shy deer bide;
While light comes pouring
Diamond-wise from her side.

Grassy glades are there
With boughs light-springing,
Where the wild herds fare
(Of these my singing!),
Like lightning flinging
Their heels on the air
Should the wind be bringing
Any hint to beware.

Swift is each spirited one
Clad in a fine fitting
Skin that shines like the sun
Of its glory unwitting.
Like a banner when they run
Of flame-red is their flitting.
A clever deed would be done
A shot in these small bellies getting.

It calls for a prime gun
In a young man's gripping
– A flint with a breach-run

DUNCAN BÀN MACINTYRE   [132

And trigger hard-clipping
On the hammer with none
Of hesitation or slipping;
A sound-stocked eight-sided one
To catch a stag skipping.

Yet one born for the game,
The man to outwit them,
Who whene'er he took aim
Was certain to hit them,
Lived here, Patrick by name,
Swiftly though when he came
With his boys and dogs they might flit them.

*

The hind loves to wander
Among the saplings yonder.
The passes of the braes
Are her dwelling-place.
The leaflets of the trees
And fresh heather-stems – these
Are the fare she prefers,
To cattle-fodder averse.
Blithe and gentle her nature,
A glad gloomless creature,
Mercurial and thoughtless,
Going like a knotless
Thread through the landscape,
Yet bearing herself always
Circumspect and comely in shape,
With the hues of health ablaze;
Knowing precisely how far to press
Her vital force to fill out,
Without straining, her formal niceness,

At rest or in revel or rout.
In the glen of the sappiest
Green copsewood she's happiest,
Yet often goes by the Great Rock
Where bush-clumps break the shock
Of the North Wind and let
No icy jet of it get
On her slumbering there
In some favourite lair;
Or she trips up the dell
Of the hazels to the well
She loves to drink at; cold and clear,
Far better than beer.
No one could think of
Better for her to drink of.
It inspires her lithe wiles,
Her sheer grace that beguiles,
Her constant strength and speed
In every hazard of need.
The honour of the best ears
In all Europe is hers!

CRUNN-LUTH

Who would stalk the hind in this glen
    Needs good knowledge and cunning
To steal softly within her ken
    Without starting her running,
Carefully and cleverly inveigling
    Himself forward, her notice shunning,
Using each least thing in turn then
    To hide himself and his gun in.
Bush, rock, and hollow all in taken,
    Vastly ingenious, there's great fun in.

Details of the land all well gauged,
　　Clouds' direction duly noted,
His wits are thenceforth all engaged
　　In covering the space allotted,
And getting the finale staged
　　Before the hind can have thought it
Enplotted – aye, all the campaign waged
　　Ere hint of danger is brought it.

The hind's own instincts outplaying,
　　In spite of herself she's taken
By the stalker, not without paying
　　Full due to her wits wide-waken,
With tribute of stilly delaying
　　And coolness never forsaken
And frame to wriggle a worm's way in
　　Without affront or aching.

At last he puts the eye steadily
　　To the hind on the stag still intent,
And the peg is drawn out readily
　　The butt-iron's kick to relent.
A new flint's just tightened, and deadly
　　The down-blow of the hammer's sent
The spark to the packed powder flies redly
　　And the hail from the barrel is sprent.

It was well loved by the quality
　　To be up Ben Dorain's passes
In the hey-day of their vitality
　　Where the deer troop by in masses,
While hunters of such judicality
　　In the sport where nothing crass is
Stalk them with the right mentality
　　That alone their wariness outclasses.

And the brisk keen dogs behind them,
    Creatures so surly and slaughtering,
Frantic at jaws' grip to find them
    With the herd like wild-fire scattering,
Till speed it seems has combined them
    – Their hair-on-end howling, shattering
The golden silence of deer-flight, entwined them
    With the foes their rabid foam's spattering.

Furious in high career that conjunction
    Of leaping dogs and fugitive deer,
And the peaks and passes echoed with unction
    The baying of the hounds exciting to hear
As they drove down their quarries without compunction
    In to the icy pools that bottomless appear
And rocked on their necks in relentless function
    While they floundered and bloodied the waters there!

... Though I've told a little of Ben Dorain here,
Before I could tell all it deserves I would be
In a delirium with the strange prolixity
Of the talking called for, I fear.

Translated from the Gaelic
by Hugh MacDiarmid

In Praise of Limestone

If it form the one landscape that we, the inconstant ones,
    Are consistently homesick for, this is chiefly
Because it dissolves in water. Mark these rounded slopes
    With their surface fragrance of thyme and, beneath,
A secret system of caves and conduits; hear the springs
    That spurt out everywhere with a chuckle,
Each filling a private pool for its fish and carving
    Its own little ravine whose cliffs entertain
The butterfly and the lizard; examine this region
    Of short distances and definite places:
What could be more like Mother or a fitter background
    For her son, the flirtatious male who lounges
Against a rock in the sunlight, never doubting
    That for all his faults he is loved; whose works are but
Extensions of his power to charm? From weathered outcrop
    To hill-top temple, from appearing waters to
Conspicuous fountains, from a wild to a formal vineyard,
    Are ingenious but short steps that a child's wish
To receive more attention than his brothers, whether
    By pleasing or teasing, can easily take.

Watch, then, the band of rivals as they climb up and down
    Their steep stone gennels in twos and threes, at times
Arm in arm, but never, thank God, in step; or engaged
    On the shady side of a square at midday in
Voluble discourse, knowing each other too well to think
    There are any important secrets, unable
To conceive a god whose temper-tantrums are moral
    And not to be pacified by a clever line
Or a good lay: for, accustomed to a stone that responds,
    They have never had to veil their faces in awe

Of a crater whose blazing fury could not be fixed;
    Adjusted to the local needs of valleys
Where everything can be touched or reached by walking,
    Their eyes have never looked into infinite space
Through the lattice-work of a nomad's comb; born lucky,
    Their legs have never encountered the fungi
And insects of the jungle, the monstrous forms and lives
    With which we have nothing, we like to hope, in common.
So, when one of them goes to the bad, the way his mind works
    Remains comprehensible: to become a pimp
Or deal in fake jewellery or ruin a fine tenor voice
    For effects that bring down the house, could happen to all
But the best and the worst of us . . .
            That is why, I suppose,
The best and worst never stayed here long but sought
Immoderate soils where the beauty was not so external,
    The light less public and the meaning of life
Something more than a mad camp. 'Come!' cried the granite
    wastes,
'How evasive is your humor, how accidental
Your kindest kiss, how permanent is death.' (Saints-to-be
    Slipped away sighing.) 'Come!' purred the clays and gravels,
'On our plains there is room for armies to drill; rivers
    Wait to be tamed and slaves to construct you a tomb
In the grand manner: soft as the earth is mankind and both
    Need to be altered.' (Intendant Caesars rose and
Left, slamming the door.) But the really reckless were fetched
    By an older colder voice, the oceanic whisper:
'I am the solitude that asks and promises nothing;
    That is how I shall set you free. There is no love;
There are only the various envies, all of them sad.'

They were right, my dear, all those voices were right
And still are; this land is not the sweet home that it looks,

Nor its peace the historical calm of a site
Where something was settled once and for all: A backward
    And dilapidated province, connected
To the big busy world by a tunnel, with a certain
    Seedy appeal, is that all it is now? Not quite:
It has a worldly duty which in spite of itself
    It does not neglect, but calls into question
All the Great Powers assume; it disturbs our rights. The poet,
    Admired for his earnest habit of calling
The sun the sun, his mind Puzzle, is made uneasy
    By these marble statues which so obviously doubt
His antimythological myth; and these gamins,
    Pursuing the scientist down the tiled colonnade
With such lively offers, rebuke his concern for Nature's
    Remotest aspects: I, too, am reproached, for what
And how much you know. Not to lose time, not to get caught,
    Not to be left behind, not, please! to resemble
The beasts who repeat themselves, or a thing like water
    Or stone whose conduct can be predicted, these
Are our Common Prayer, whose greatest comfort is music
    Which can be made anywhere, is invisible,
And does not smell. In so far as we have to look forward
    To death as a fact, no doubt we are right: But if
Sins can be forgiven, if bodies rise from the dead,
    These modifications of matter into
Innocent athletes and gesticulating fountains,
    Made solely for pleasure, make a further point:
The blessed will not care what angle they are regarded from,
    Having nothing to hide. Dear, I know nothing of
Either, but when I try to imagine a faultless love
    Or the life to come, what I hear is the murmur
Of underground streams, what I see is a limestone landscape.

Benedicite

[*from* The Book of Common Prayer]

O all ye Works of the Lord, bless ye the Lord:
praise him, and magnify him for ever.

O ye Angels of the Lord, bless ye the Lord:
praise him, and magnify him for ever.

O ye Heavens, bless ye the Lord:
praise him, and magnify him for ever.

O ye Waters that be above the Firmament, bless ye the Lord:
praise him, and magnify him for ever.

O all ye Powers of the Lord, bless ye the Lord:
praise him, and magnify him for ever.

O ye Sun and Moon, bless ye the Lord:
praise him, and magnify him for ever.

O ye Stars of Heaven, bless ye the Lord:
praise him, and magnify him for ever.

O ye Showers and Dew, bless ye the Lord:
praise him, and magnify him for ever.

O ye Winds of God, bless ye the Lord:
praise him, and magnify him for ever.

O ye Fire and Heat, bless ye the Lord:
praise him, and magnify him for ever.

O ye Winter and Summer, bless ye the Lord:
praise him, and magnify him for ever.

O ye Dews and Frosts, bless ye the Lord:
praise him, and magnify him for ever.

O ye Frost and Cold, bless ye the Lord:
praise him, and magnify him for ever.

O ye Ice and Snow, bless ye the Lord:
praise him, and magnify him for ever.

O ye Nights and Days, bless ye the Lord:
praise him, and magnify him for ever.

O ye Light and Darkness, bless ye the Lord:
praise him, and magnify him for ever.

O ye Lightnings and Clouds, bless ye the Lord:
praise him, and magnify him for ever.

O let the Earth bless the Lord:
yea, let it praise him, and magnify him for ever.

O ye Mountains and Hills, bless ye the Lord:
praise him, and magnify him for ever.

O all ye Green Things upon the Earth, bless ye the Lord:
praise him, and magnify him for ever.

O ye Wells, bless ye the Lord:
praise him, and magnify him for ever.

O ye Seas and Floods, bless ye the Lord:
praise him, and magnify him for ever.

O ye Whales, and all that move in the Waters, bless ye the Lord:
praise him, and magnify him for ever.

O all ye Fowls of the Air, bless ye the Lord:
praise him, and magnify him for ever.

O all ye Beasts and Cattle, bless ye the Lord:
praise him, and magnify him for ever.

O ye Children of Men, bless ye the Lord:
praise him, and magnify him for ever.

O let Israel bless the Lord:
praise him, and magnify him for ever.

O ye Priests of the Lord, bless ye the Lord:
praise him, and magnify him for ever.

O ye Servants of the Lord, bless ye the Lord:
praise him, and magnify him for ever.

O ye Spirits and Souls of the Righteous, bless ye the Lord:
praise him, and magnify him for ever.

O ye holy and humble Men of heart, bless ye the Lord:
praise him, and magnify him for ever.

O Ananias, Azarias and Misael, bless ye the Lord:
praise him, and magnify him for ever.

Glory be to the Father, and to the Son:
and to the Holy Ghost;
as it was in the beginning, is now, and ever shall be:
world without end. Amen.

Song of a Hebrew

A jazz poem

Working is another way of praying.
You plant in Israel the soul of a tree.
You plant in the desert the spirit of gardens.

Praying is another way of singing.
You plant in the tree the soul of lemons.
You plant in the gardens the spirit of roses.

Singing is another way of loving.
You plant in the lemons the spirit of your son.
You plant in the roses the soul of your daughter.

Loving is another way of living.
You plant in your daughter the spirit of Israel.
You plant in your son the soul of the desert.

Mowing

There was never a sound beside the wood but one,
And that was my long scythe whispering to the ground.
What was it it whispered? I knew not well myself;
Perhaps it was something about the heat of the sun,
Something, perhaps, about the lack of sound –
And that was why it whispered and did not speak.
It was no dream of the gift of idle hours,
Or easy gold at the hand of fay or elf:
Anything more than the truth would have seemed too weak
To the earnest love that laid the swale in rows,
Not without feeble-pointed spikes of flowers
(Pale orchises), and scared a bright green snake.
The fact is the sweetest dream that labor knows.
My long scythe whispered and left the hay to make.

'If you see my mother'

(A work song sung by Negro prisoners in Texas to accompany group work like cotton-picking or sugar-cane-cutting, and recorded in 1964. The collector writes: 'This is another of those songs that are too anguished to come through on a printed page. The words are simple, the tune sometimes becomes no more than a moan, then the moan becomes words again.')

If you see my mother, partner, tell her pray for me,
I got life on the river, yeah, never will go free, never will go free.

They 'cuse me a murder,
Never harmed a man, never harmed a man.

I say wake up ol' dead man,
Help me carry my row, help me carry my row.

Well the row so grassy,
I can hardly go, I can hardly go.

MACK MAZE

Mississippi Bo Weavil Blues

It's a little bo weavil she's movin' in the . . . lordie
You can plant your cotton and you won't get a half a cent, lordie
Bo weavil bo weavil, where's your native home? lordie
'A-Louisiana leavin' Texas anywhere I'se bred and born,' lordie
Well I saw the bo weavil lord a circle lordie in the air, lordie
The next time I seed him lord he had his family there, lordie
Bo Weavil left Texas lord he bid me 'Fare thee well', lordie
('where you goin' now?')
'I'm goin' down to the Mississippi, gonna give Louisiana (hell)',
    lordie
Bo weavil said to the farmer: 'Ain't got ticket fare', lordie
('How is that, boy?')
Sucks all the blossom and he leave your hedges square, lordie
An' the next time I seed you you know you had your family there,
    lordie
Bo weavil (met) his wife: 'We can sit down on the hill', lordie
Bo weavil told his wife: 'Let's take this forty here,' lordie
Bo weavil told his wife says: 'I believe I may go north', lordie
(Hold on, I'm gonna tell all about that)
Let's live in (leavin') Louisiana we can go to Arkansas', lordie
Well I saw the bo weavil lord a circle lord in the air, lordie
Next time I seed him lord he had his family there, lordie
Bo weavil told the farmer that 'I ain't got ticket fare', lordie
Sucks all the blossom and leave your hedges square, lordie
Bo weavil bo weavil, where your native home? lordie
'Most anywhere they raise cotton and corn', lordie
'Bo weavil bo weavil, oughta (gonna) treat me fair', lordie
'The next time I did you had your family there', lordie.

Landscape

In the ennui unending
of the flat land
the vague snow descending
shines like sand.

With no gleam of light
in the copper sky,
one imagines he might
see the moon live and die.

In the nearby woods
among the mist
gray oaks twist
like floating clouds.

With no gleam of light
in the copper sky,
one imagines he might
see the moon live and die.

Wind-broken crow,
and starving wolves too,
when sharp winds blow
what happens to you?

In the ennui unending
of the flat land
the vague snow descending
shines like sand.

*Translated from the French
by C. F. Macintyre*

PAUL VERLAINE

Tam Snow

to Kaye Webb

Who in the bleak wood
Barefoot, ice-fingered,
Runs to and fro?
   Tam Snow.

Who, soft as a ghost,
Falls on our house to strike
Blow after blow?
   Tam Snow.

Who with a touch of the hand
Stills the world's sound
In its flow?
   Tam Snow.

Who holds to our side,
Though as friend or as foe
We never may know?
   Tam Snow.

Who hides in the hedge
After thaw, waits for more
Of his kind to show?
   Tam Snow.

Who is the guest
First we welcome, then
Long to see go?
   Tam Snow.

Snow and Snow

Snow is sometimes a she, a soft one.
   Her kiss on your cheek, her finger on your sleeve
In early December, on a warm evening,
   And you turn to meet her, saying 'It's snowing!'
      But it is not. And nobody's there.
      Empty and calm is the air.

Sometimes the snow is a he, a sly one.
   Weakly he signs the dry stone with a damp spot.
Waifish he floats and touches the pond and is not.
   Treacherous-beggarly he falters, and taps at the window.
      A little longer he clings to the grass-blade tip
      Getting his grip.

Then how she leans, how furry foxwrap she nestles
   The sky with her warm, and the earth with her softness.
How her lit crowding fairytales sink through the space-silence
   To build her palace, till it twinkles in starlight –
      Too frail for a foot
      Or a crumb of soot.

Then how his muffled armies move in all night
   And we wake and every road is blockaded
Every hill taken and every farm occupied
   And the white glare of his tents is on the ceiling.
      And all that dull blue day and on into the gloaming
      We have to watch more coming.

Then everything in the rubbish-heaped world
   Is a bridesmaid at her miracle.
Dunghills and crumbly dark old barns are bowed in the chapel of
   her sparkle,

The gruesome boggy cellars of the wood
    Are a wedding of lace
    Now taking place.

from Sweeney Astray
[The Trees of Ireland]

The bushy leafy oak tree
is highest in the wood,
the forking shoots of hazel
hide sweet hazel-nuts.

The alder is my darling,
all thornless in the gap,
some milk of human kindness
coursing in its sap.

The blackthorn is a jaggy creel
stippled with dark sloes;
green watercress in thatch on wells
where the drinking blackbird goes.

Sweetest of the leafy stalks,
the vetches strew the pathway;
the oyster-grass is my delight
and the wild strawberry.

Low-set clumps of apple trees
drum down fruit when shaken;
scarlet berries clot like blood
on mountain rowan.

Briars curl in sideways,
arch a stickle back,
draw blood and curl up innocent
to sneak the next attack.

SEAMUS HEANEY

The yew tree in each churchyard
wraps night in its dark hood.
Ivy is a shadowy
genius of the wood.

Holly rears its windbreak,
a door in winter's face;
life-blood on a spear-shaft
darkens the grain of ash.

Birch tree, smooth and blessed,
delicious to the breeze,
high twigs plait and crown it
the queen of trees.

The aspen pales
and whispers, hesitates:
a thousand frightened scuts
race in its leaves.

But what disturbs me the most
in the leafy wood
is the to and fro and to and fro
of an oak rod.

[The Woodman,
or the Beauties of a Winter Forest]

Now 'tis winter! plainly shewn by the icicles which hang pendant from the low mossy eaves of the woodmans cottage – who now with his mattocks and leather doublet is ready to begin his winters labour; to cut down the wood in the still forest and plash the hedge to stand as a fence to the intruding cattle, – He and he only knows and sees the beauties and horrors of winter mingled together through the short day – For the shepherd cuts his journeys short and now only visits his flock on necessity . . . Croodling with his hands in his pockets and his crook under his arm he tramples the frosty plain with dithering haste; glad and eager to return to the warm corner of his cottage fire – His favorite tree (where he was wont in summer to stretch his limbs in idle dalliance on the flowery turf beneath its cooling shade) is now left desolate rob'd both of its idle shepherd and the green foliage that cloth'd its summer boughs – The milk-boy too in his morning rambles no longer saunters to the pasture as he had used to do in summer (pausing on every pathway flower and swanking idly along, often staring with open mouth thoughtlessly musing on the heavens as if he could wish for something in the passing clouds; leaning his lazy sides 'gainst every stile he come to, and can never get his heavy clouted shoon over the lowest without resting; sighing as he retires with the deepest regret to leave such easy chairs) – But now in hasty claumping tread finding nothing but cold and snow to pause on, he never stops to [?cawm] his thoughtless head about – but shuffling along he makes the frosty plain reecho with his hasty bruzzing foot steps – the stiles which were so hard to climb over in summer are now scal'd with the greatest ease and he wishes for nothing but his journeys end – prefering the sheltering warm confines of the farmyard and Stables before the frozen plain – But 'tis not so with the woodman no he glories in the weather! and rising early in the dark morning ere the copper color'd streaks appear to spread over the eastern sky – he pursues his journey over many new made hills and valleys of new fallen snow with 'heart felt glee' cheering the rugged way with the oft-repeated scrap of an harmless old song making the rhymy-feather'd thickets resond in rural melody –

Sonnet, made upon the Groves near *Merlou* Castle

You well compacted Groves, whose light and shade
   Mixt equally, produce nor heat, nor cold,
   Either to burn the young, or freeze the old,
But to one even temper being made,
Upon a greene embroidering through each Glade
   An Airy Silver, and a Sunny Gold,
   So cloath the poorest that they do behold
Themselves, in riches which can never fade,
   While the wind whistles, and the birds do sing,
While your twigs clip, and while the leaves do friss,
   While the fruit ripens which those trunks do bring,
   Sensless to all but love, do you not spring
Pleasure of such a kind, as truly is
A self-renewing vegetable bliss.

'How long does it take to make the woods?'

How long does it take to make the woods?
As long as it takes to make the world.
The woods is present as the world is, the presence
of all its past and of all its time to come.
It is always finished, it is always being made, the act
of its making forever greater than the act of its destruction.
It is a part of eternity, for its end and beginning
belong to the end and beginning of all things,
the beginning lost in the end, the end in the beginning.

What is the way to the woods, how do you get there?
By climbing up through the six days' field,
kept in all the body's years, the body's
sorrow, weariness and joy, by passing through
the narrow gate on the far side of that field
where the pasture grass of the body's life gives way
to the high original standing of the trees.
By coming into the shadow, the shadow
of the grace of the straight way's ending,
the shadow of the mercy of light.

Why must the gate be narrow?
Because you cannot pass beyond it burdened.
To come into the woods you must leave behind
the six days' world, all of it, all of its plans and hopes.
You must come without weapon or tool, alone,
expecting nothing, remembering nothing,
into the ease of sight, the brotherhood of eye and leaf.

Glimpse

'O leaves,' Crow sang, trembling, 'O leaves –'

The touch of a leaf's edge at his throat
Guillotined further comment.

                              Nevertheless
Speechless he continued to stare at the leaves

Through the god's head instantly substituted.

from Mavria

Enter Anna and Doina and three Carnival characters, the Moroccan King, Doctor Ironbeard and the Corporal, chasing the worn-out Tree King, Stefan following. The King is dressed in bark and covered with flowers.

KING: Mercy, mercy!

ANNA: Not from me!

DOINA: Hit him with a piece of tree!

ANNA: The betrayer is betrayed,
With the stuff from which he's made.

ALL CARNIVAL PEOPLE: We have chased him from the wood
Where for ages he had stood,
Giving orders to the flowers,
And enjoying royal powers.
Through the undergrowth we came,
Crying out his secret name,
And he lifted up his roots,
And in terror off he shoots!
Through the light and through the shade,
Through the sun-uplifted glade,
With his saplings crying, 'Run,
Father, faster than the sun!'
But we changed into a deer
And he pissed himself in fear,
And we changed into a hare
And he soiled his underwear,
And we changed into a hound,
And he dribbled on the ground,
And we changed into a bird

PETER OSWALD   [158

And his bowels could be heard.
And we changed into a shirt,
And we told him, 'This won't hurt!'
He ran down a railway line
Like a shiver down a spine,
Like a painting in the rain,
Or a dripping window pane,
Like a sweater, like a sore,
Like mascara on a whore,
Like mascara on a widow;
And we changed into a meadow –

Enter Judge and Executioner.

JUDGE: Stop! You have run on too long
With your silly little song.
Now his Majesty must be
Judged impartially by me.
Tell me, what have been his crimes?

DOCTOR IRONBEARD: He has dripped a thousand times
Down my neck, which made me squirm.

CORPORAL: He gave comfort to a worm.

MOROCCAN KING: And he hid an outlawed bird
That was taken at its word.

CORPORAL: Ask him where his children are,
Whom he scattered near and far
From September to December.

JUDGE: Do you know?

KING:　　　　　I can't remember.

JUDGE: Have you anything to say?

KING: Gentle friends, from March to May
I grew greater, and I bore,
Through the summer, more and more
Heavy leaves to give you shade,
And beneath my boughs you laid
Down your sorrows, and each other.
Many there became a mother.
And you turn against me now,
For no reason, like a sow
Lying on her squealing litter.
Life is sweet, but death is bitter.
Tell the bluebell I adore
That her lover is no more.
Tell her, oh sweet people, tell her
That her summergreen umbrella
Is a boat, a blaze, a table.
To speak more I am unable.

JUDGE: Sentimental tripe and dribble.
What's the verdict on old Stilty?
Guilty?

DOCTOR IRONBEARD: Guilty.

CORPORAL: Guilty.

MOROCCAN KING: Guilty.

JUDGE: Weeping log, I sentence you
To be cut at once in two.
Fell him, executioner!

EXECUTIONER: People ought to call me sir.

*Shaking his head, the Executioner places three or more hats on top of
each other on the King's head. The others count.*

OTHERS: One, two, three –

from In Parenthesis

The trees are very high in the wan signal-beam, for whose slow gyration their wounded boughs seem as malignant limbs, manœuvring for advantage.

The trees of the wood beware each other
                    and under each a man sitting;
their seemly faces as carved in a sardonyx stone; as undiademed princes turn their gracious profiles in a hidden seal, so did these appear, under the changing light.

For that waning you would believe this flaxen head had for its
    broken pedestal these bent Silurian shoulders.

For the pale flares extinction you don't know if under his close lids, his eye-balls watch you. You would say by the turn of steel at his wide brow he is not of our men where he leans with his open fist in Dai's bosom against the White Stone.

Hung so about, you make between these your close escape.

The secret princes between the leaning trees have diadems given them.

Life the leveller hugs her impudent equality – she may proceed at once to less discriminating zones.

The Queen of the Woods has cut bright boughs of various flowering.

These knew her influential eyes. Her awarding hands can pluck for each their fragile prize.

She speaks to them according to precedence. She knows what's due to this elect society. She can choose twelve gentle-men. She knows who is most lord between the high trees and on the open down.

Some she gives white berries
                    some she gives brown

DAVID JONES   [161

Emil has a curious crown it's
              made of golden saxifrage.

Fatty wears sweet-briar,
he will reign with her for a thousand years.

For Balder she reaches high to fetch his.

Ulrich smiles for his myrtle wand.

That swine Lillywhite has daisies to his chain – you'd hardly credit it.

She plaits torques of equal splendour for Mr Jenkins and Billy Crower.

Hansel with Gronwy share dog-violets for a palm, where they lie in serious embrace beneath the twisted tripod.

Siôn gets St John's Wort – that's fair enough.

Dai Great-coat, she can't find him anywhere – she calls both high and low, she had a very special one for him.

Among this July noblesse she is mindful of December wood – when the trees of the forest beat against each other because of him.

She carries to Aneirin-in-the-nullah a rowan sprig, for the glory of Guenedota. You couldn't hear what she said to him, because she was careful for the Disciplines of the Wars.

At the gate of the wood you try a last adjustment, but slung so, it's an impediment, it's of detriment to your hopes, you had best be rid of it – the sagging webbing and all and what's left of your two fifty – but it were wise to hold on to your mask.

You're clumsy in your feebleness, you implicate your tin-hat rim with the slack sling of it.

Let it lie for the dews to rust it, or ought you to decently cover the working parts.

Its dark barrel, where you leave it under the oak, reflects the solemn star that rises urgently from Cliff Trench.

It's a beautiful doll for us
it's the Last Reputable Arm.

But leave it – under the oak.
leave it for a Cook's tourist to the Devastated Areas and crawl as far
   as you can and wait for the bearers.

Mrs Willy Hartington has learned to draw sheets and so has
Miss Melpomené; and on the south lawns,
men walk in red white and blue
under the cedars
and by every green tree
and beside comfortable waters.

But why dont the bastards come –
Bearers! – stret-cher bear-errs!
or do they divide the spoils at the Aid-Post.

   But how many men do you suppose could bear away a third
of us:
drag just a little further – he yet may counter-attack.

Lie still under the oak
next to the Jerry
and Sergeant Jerry Coke.

   The feet of the reserves going up tread level with your forehead;
and no word for you; they whisper one with another; pass
on, inward;
these latest succours:
green Kimmerii to bear up the war.

Oeth and Annoeth's hosts they were
who in that night grew
younger men
younger striplings.

The geste says this and the man who was on the field . . . and who
wrote the book . . . the man who does not know this has not
understood anything.

The Poplar-Field

The poplars are fell'd, farewell to the shade
And the whispering sound of the cool colonnade,
The winds play no longer, and sing in the leaves,
Nor Ouse on his bosom their image receives.

Twelve years have elaps'd since I last took a view
Of my favourite field and the bank where they grew,
And now in the grass behold they are laid,
And the tree is my seat that once lent me a shade.

The blackbird has fled to another retreat
Where the hazels afford him a screen from the heat,
And the scene where his melody charm'd me before,
Resounds with his sweet-flowing ditty no more.

My fugitive years are all hasting away,
And I must ere long lie as lowly as they,
With a turf on my breast, and a stone at my head,
Ere another such grove shall arise in its stead.

'Tis a sight to engage me, if any thing can,
To muse on the perishing pleasures of man;
Though his life be a dream, his enjoyments, I see,
Have a being less durable even than he.

WILLIAM COWPER

from Easter Rex

(after The Dream of the Rood, *whose earliest shorter version is carved in Anglo-Saxon runes on a stone church cross, thus really suffering the tree to speak)*

i thought to me i saw the strangest tree
lifting in the sky with lustre wound about
strong ceiling beam, solid sailing boom, gold gleaming beacon
five gems stood at the axis of the limbs.
that was no felon's gallows, standing proud and flushed
through skin of gold i saw drip gore.
sorry with worry i watched clothing and colour
alter and flicker, heard speak, how hewn at the holt's end,
stirred from her stem she stood then 'that the lord of mankind
who marches up my hill might mount me.
i didn't dare break down or bend against his will.
strong for the object, the young hero, his gear stripped off,
climbed up into the greenery, heartened by the crowd,
keen to continue kind of course,
i shuddered as he held me.
i didn't dare break down or bend against the ground.
stand fast i should as a rod reared up.
i didn't dare stoop or stumble.
they drove me through with dark nails. my mark is scar-clear,
invidiously opened. i was all with blood bestreamed,
got from that man's side after he'd shot out his ghost.
many, on that mount, crude deeds of wyrd i bode.
the glow in the gloom, cloud-shadow crushed,
wan the welkin. royalty ruled by the rood.
we three crosses stayed weeping in our places
a good while after sky had soaked up the soldiers' song.
christ's corpse was cold.

RUSKIN WATTS

felled as a forest from the hill,
rough and tumbled in our pit,
girt with bright gold and silver . . .'

The Steeple-Jack

Dürer would have seen a reason for living
    in a town like this, with eight stranded whales
to look at; with the sweet sea air coming into your house
on a fine day, from water etched
    with waves as formal as the scales
on a fish.

One by one, in two's, in three's, the seagulls keep
    flying back and forth over the town clock,
or sailing around the lighthouse without moving the wings –
rising steadily with a slight
    quiver of the body – or flock
mewing where

a sea the purple of the peacock's neck is
    paled to greenish azure as Dürer changed
the pine green of the Tyrol to peacock blue and guinea
grey. You can see a twenty-five-
    pound lobster and fish-nets arranged
to dry. The

whirlwind fife-and-drum of the storm bends the salt
    marsh grass, disturbs stars in the sky and the
star on the steeple; it is a privilege to see so
much confusion.

        A steeple-jack in red, has let
    a rope down as a spider spins a thread;
he might be part of a novel, but on the sidewalk a
sign says C. J. Poole, Steeple-jack,
    in black and white; and one in red
and white says

Danger. The church portico has four fluted
    columns, each a single piece of stone, made
modester by white-wash. This would be a fit haven for
waifs, children, animals, prisoners,
    and presidents who have repaid
sin-driven

senators by not thinking about them. One
    sees a school-house, a post-office in a
store, fish-houses, hen-houses, a three-masted schooner on
the stocks. The hero, the student,
    the steeple-jack, each in his way,
is at home.

It could not be dangerous to be living
    in a town like this, of simple people,
who have a steeple-jack placing danger signs by the church
while he is gilding the solid-
    pointed star, which on a steeple
stands for hope.

The ascent of the lark is
invisible mending.

The Thrush

Music of a thrush, clearbright
Lovable language of light,
Heard I under a birchtree
Yesterday, all grace and glee –
Was ever so sweet a thing
Fine-plaited as his whistling?

Matins, he reads the lesson,
A chasuble of plumage on.
His cry from a grove, his brightshout
Over countrysides rings out,
Hill prophet, maker of moods,
Passion's bright bard of glenwoods.
Every voice of the brookside
Sings he, in his darling pride,
Every sweet-metred love-ode,
Every song and organ mode,
Competing for a truelove,
Every catch for woman's love.
Preacher and reader of lore,
Sweet and clear, inspired rapture,
Bard of Ovid's faultless rhyme,
Chief prelate mild of Springtime.

From his birch, where lovers throng,
Author of the wood's birdsong,
Merrily the glade re-echoes –
Rhymes and metres of love he knows.
He on hazel sings so well
Through cloistered trees (winged angel)
Hardly a bird of Eden

DAFYDD AP GWILYM

Had by rote remembered then
How to recite what headlong
Passion made him do with song.

*Translated from the Welsh
by Tony Conran*

The Melodious Lady-Lord

Who is she the Melodious Lady-Lord,
At the base of the knoll,
At the mouth of the wave?

Not the alc
Not the duck
Not the swan
And not alone is she.

Who is she the Melodious Lady-Lord,
At the base of the knoll,
At the mouth of the wave?

Not the lark
Not the merle
Not the mavis
On the bough is she.

Who is she the Melodious Lady-Lord,
At the base of the knoll,
At the mouth of the wave?

Not the murmuring ptarmigan
Of the hill is she.

Who is she the Melodious Lady-Lord,
At the base of the knoll,
At the mouth of the wave?

Not the grilse of the stream
Not the seal of the wave
Not the sea maiden
Of May is she.

ANONYMOUS

Who is she the Melodious Lady-Lord
At the base of the knoll,
At the mouth of the wave?

Not the dame of the distaff
Not the damsel of the lyre
Not the golden-haired maid
Of the flocks is she.

Who is she the Melodious Lady-Lord
At the base of the knoll,
At the mouth of the wave?

Melodious Lady-Lord
God-like in loveliness.

Daughter of a King
Grand-daughter of a King
Great grand-daughter of a King
Great great grand-daughter of a King
Great great great grand-daughter of a King
Wife of a King
Mother of a King
Foster mother of a King
She lullabying a King
And he under her plaid.

From Erin she travelled
For Lochlann is bound.
May the Trinity travel with her
Withersoever she goes
Withersoever she goes.

Three Riddles

ICE

The wave, over the wave a weird thing I saw
through wrought and wonderfully ornate,
a wonder on the wave, water became bone.

Translated from the Old English
by Michael Alexander

WAVES

Who are the women who hurry round the skerries
Then take a long trip down the firth?
Their beds are hard, their hoods are white,
And they cannot play in the calm.

Translated from the Old Norse
by W. H. Auden

SNOW

A white bird floats down through the air
and never a tree but he lights there.

Translated from the Old English
by Geoffrey Grigson

ANONYMOUS

John Barleycorn

There were three men came out of the west
Their fortunes for to try,
And these three men made a solemn vow
John Barleycorn should die.

They've ploughed, they've sown, they've harrowed him in,
Throw'd clods upon his head,
And these three men made a solemn vow
John Barleycorn was dead.

They've let him lie for a very long time
Till the rain from heaven did fall,
Then little Sir John sprung up his head
And soon amazed them all.

They've let him stand till Midsummer Day
Till he looked both pale and wan,
And little Sir John's grown a long, long beard
And so become a man.

They've hired men with their scythes so sharp
To cut him off at the knee,
They've rolled and tied him by the waist,
Serving him most barb'rously.

They've hired men with their sharp pitch forks
Who pricked him to the heart,
And the loader he served him worse than that
For he's bound him to the cart.

They've wheeled him round and around the field
Till they came unto the barn
And there they've made a solemn mow
Of poor John Barleycorn.

ANONYMOUS [175

They've hired men with the crabtree sticks
To cut him skin from bone,
And the miller he has served him worse than that
For he's ground him between two stones.

Here's little Sir John in the nut brown bowl
And here's brandy in the glass,
And little Sir John in the nut brown bowl
Proved the strongest man at last

For the huntsman he can't hunt the fox
And so loudly blow his horn
And the tinker he can't mend kettles nor pots
Without a little barleycorn.

Cynddylan on a Tractor

Ah, you should see Cynddylan on a tractor.
Gone the old look that yoked him to the soil;
He's a new man now, part of the machine,
His nerves of metal and his blood oil.
The clutch curses, but the gears obey
His least bidding, and lo, he's away
Out of the farmyard, scattering hens.
Riding to work now as a great man should,
He is the knight at arms breaking the fields'
Mirror of silence, emptying the wood
Of foxes and squirrels and bright jays.
The sun comes over the tall trees
Kindling all the hedges, but not for him
Who runs his engine on a different fuel.
And all the birds are singing, bills wide in vain,
As Cynddylan passes proudly up the lane.

The Shield of Archilles

[*From* The Iliad]

To these the fierie Artizan did adde a new-ear'd field,
Large and thrice plowd, the soyle being soft and of a wealthy
    yeeld;
And many men at plow he made that drave earth here and there
And turnd up stitches orderly; at whose end when they were,
A fellow ever gave their hands full cups of luscious wine,
Which emptied, for another stitch the earth they undermine,
And long till th' utmost bound be reacht of all the ample Close.
The soyle turnd up behind the plow, all blacke like earth arose,
Though forg'd of nothing else but gold, and lay in show as light
As if it had bene plowd indeed, miraculous to sight.

There grew by this a field of corne, high, ripe, where reapers
    wrought,
And let thicke handfuls fall to earth, for which some other
    brought
Bands, and made sheaves. Three binders stood and tooke the
    handfuls reapt
From boyes that gatherd quickly up, and by them armefuls heapt.
Amongst these at a furrowe's end the king stood pleasd at heart,
Said no word, but his scepter shewd. And from him, much apart,
His harvest Bailiffes underneath an Oke a feast prepar'd,
And, having kild a mightie Oxe, stood there to see him shar'd,
Which women for their harvest folks (then come to sup) had
    drest,
And many white wheate-cakes bestow'd, to make it up a feast.

He set neare this a vine of gold that crackt beneath the weight
Of bunches blacke with being ripe; to keepe which, at the height,
A silver raile ranne all along, and round about it flow'd

An azure mote, and to this guard a quick-set was bestow'd
Of Tin, one onely path to all, by which the pressemen came
In time of vintage: youths and maids, that bore not yet the flame
Of manly Hymen, baskets bore of grapes and mellow fruite.
A lad that sweetly toucht a harpe, to which his voice did suite,
Centerd the circles of that youth, all whose skill could not do
The wanton's pleasure to their minds, that danc't, sung, whistl'd
    too.

A herd of Oxen then he carv'd with high-raisd heads, forg'd all
Of Gold and Tin (for colour mixt), and bellowing from their stall
Rusht to their pastures at a flood, that eccho'd all their throtes,
Exceeding swift and full of reeds. And all in yellow cotes,
Foure heardsmen follow'd; after whom nine Mastives went.
    In head
Of all the heard, upon a Bull, that deadly bellowed,
Two horrid Lions rampt, and seisd, and tugg'd off bellowing still.
Both men and dogs came, yet they tore the hide and lapt their fill
Of blacke blood, and the entrailes eate. In vaine the men assayd
To set their dogs on: none durst pinch, but curre-like stood and
    bayd
In both the faces of their kings, and all their onsets fled.

Then in a passing pleasant vale the famous Artsman fed
(Upon a goodly pasture ground) rich flocks of white-fleec't sheepe,
Built stables, cottages and cotes, that did the sheapheards keepe

From winde and weather. Next to these he cut a dancing place
All full of turnings, that was like the admirable maze
For faire-hair'd Ariadne made by cunning Dædalus;
And in it youths and virgins danc't, all yong and beautious,
And glewed in another's palmes. Weeds that the winde did tosse
The virgines wore, the youths, woven cotes that cast a faint dimme
    glosse,

Like that of oyle. Fresh garlands too the virgines' temples crownd;
The youths guilt swords wore at their thighs, with silver bawdricks
    bound.
Sometimes all wound close in a ring, to which as fast they spunne
As any wheele a Turner makes, being tried how it will runne
While he is set; and out againe, as full of speed, they wound,
Not one left fast or breaking hands. A multitude stood round,
Delighted with their nimble sport: to end which, two begun
(Mids all) a song, and, turning, sung the sport's conclusion.
All this he circl'd in the shield, with pouring round about
(In all his rage) the Ocean, that it might never out.

Translated from the Greek
by George Chapman

Threshing Morning

On an apple-ripe September morning
Through the mist-chill fields I went
With a pitchfork on my shoulder
Less for use than for devilment.

The threshing mill was set-up, I knew,
In Cassidy's haggard last night,
And we owed them a day at the threshing
Since last year. O it was delight

To be paying bills of laughter
And chaffy gossip in kind
With work thrown in to ballast
The fantasy-soaring mind.

As I crossed the wooden bridge I wondered
As I looked into the drain
If ever a summer morning should find me
Shovelling up eels again.

And I thought of the wasps' nest in the bank
And how I got chased one day
Leaving the drag and the scraw-knife behind,
How I covered my face with hay.

The wet leaves of the cocksfoot
Polished my boots as I
Went round by the glistening bog-holes
Lost in unthinking joy.

I'll be carrying bags today, I mused,
The best job at the mill

With plenty of time to talk of our loves
As we wait for the bags to fill . . .

Maybe Mary might call round . . .
And then I came to the haggard gate,
And I knew as I entered that I had come
Through fields that were part of no earthly estate.

Cowslips and Larks

I hear it said yon land is poor,
In spite of those rich cowslips there –
And all the singing larks it shoots
To heaven from the cowslips' roots.
But I, with eyes that beauty find,
And music ever in my mind,
Feed my thoughts well upon that grass
Which starves the horse, the ox, and ass.
So here I stand, two miles to come
To Shapwick and my ten-days-home,
Taking my summer's joy, although
The distant clouds are dark and low,
And comes a storm that, fierce and strong,
Has brought the Mendip Hills along:
Those hills that, when the light is there,
Are many a sunny mile from here.

from The Legend of Good Women

Now have I thanne eek this condicioun,
That, of al the floures in the mede,
Thanne love I most thise floures white and rede,
Swiche as men callen daysyes in our toun.
To hem have I so gret affeccioun,
As I seyde erst, whanne comen is the May,
That in my bed ther daweth me no day
That I nam up and walkyng in the mede
To seen this flour ayein the sonne sprede,
Whan it upryseth erly by the morwe. [. . .]

My besy gost, that thursteth alwey newe
To seen this flour so yong, so fressh of hewe,
Constreyned me with so gledy desir
That in myn herte I feele yet the fir
That made me to ryse er yt were day –
And this was now the firste morwe of May –
With dredful hert and glad devocioun,
For to ben at the resureccioun
Of this flour, whan that yt shulde unclose
Agayn the sonne, that roos as red as rose,
That in the brest was of the beste, that day,
That Agenores doghtre ladde away.
And doun on knes anoon-ryght I me sette,
And, as I koude, this fresshe flour I grette,
Knelyng alwey, til it unclosed was,
Upon the smale, softe, swote gras, [. . .]

Adoun ful softely I gan to synke,
And, lenynge on myn elbowe and my syde,

The longe day I shoop me for t'abide
For nothing elles, and I shal nat lye,
But for to loke upon the dayesie,
That wel by reson men it calle may
The 'dayesye,' or elles the 'ye of day,'
The emperice and flour of floures alle [. . .]

    Whan that the sonne out of the south gan weste,
And that this flour gan close and goon to reste
For derknesse of the nyght, the which she dredde,
Hom to myn hous ful swiftly I me spedde
To goon to reste, and erly for to ryse,
To seen this flour to sprede, as I devyse.
And in a litel herber that I have,
That benched was on turves fressh ygrave,
I bad men sholde me my couche make;
For deyntee of the newe someres sake,
I bad hem strawen floures on my bed.
Whan I was leyd and had myn eyen hed,
I fel on slepe within an houre or twoo.
Me mette how I lay in the medewe thoo,
To seen this flour that I so love and drede;
And from afer com walkyng in the mede
The god of Love, and in his hand a quene,
And she was clad in real habit grene.
A fret of gold she hadde next her heer,
And upon that a whit corowne she beer
With flourouns smale, and I shal nat lye;
For al the world, ryght as a dayesye
Ycorouned ys with white leves lyte,
So were the flowrouns of hire coroune white.
For of o perle fyn, oriental,
Hire white coroune was ymaked al;

For which the white coroune above the grene
Made hire lyk a daysie for to sene,
Considered eke hir fret of gold above.

The Clote

(Water-Lily)

O zummer clote! when the brook's a-glidèn
　　So slow an' smooth down his zedgy bed,
Upon thy broad leaves so seäfe a-ridèn
　　The water's top wi' thy yollow head,
　　　　By alder's heads, O,
　　　　An' bulrush beds, O,
Thou then dost float, goolden zummer clote!

The grey-bough'd withy's a-leänèn lowly
　　Above the water thy leaves do hide;
The bendèn bulrush, a-swaÿèn slowly,
　　Do skirt in zummer thy river's zide;
　　　　An' perch in shoals, O,
　　　　Do vill the holes, O,
Where thou dost float, goolden zummer clote!

Oh! when thy brook-drinkèn flow'r's a-blowèn,
　　The burnèn zummer's a-zettèn in;
The time o' greenness, the time o' mowèn,
　　When in the haÿ-vield, wi' zunburnt skin,
　　　　The vo'k do drink, O,
　　　　Upon the brink, O,
Where thou dost float, goolden zummer clote!

Wi' eärms a-spreadèn, an' cheäks a-blowèn,
　　How proud wer I when I vu'st could zwim
Athirt the pleäce where thou bist a-growèn,
　　Wi' thy long more vrom the bottom dim;
　　　　While cows, knee-high, O,
　　　　In brook, wer nigh, O,
Where thou dost float, goolden zummer clote!

WILLIAM BARNES

Ov all the brooks drough the meäds a-windèn,
  Ov all the meäds by a river's brim,
There's nwone so feäir o' my own heart's vindèn,
  As where the maïdens do zee thee zwim,
    An' stan' to teäke, O,
      Wi' long-stemm'd reäke, O,
Thy flow'r afloat, goolden zummer clote!

Prothalamion

1

Calme was the day, and through the trembling ayre,
Sweete breathing *Zephyrus* did softly play
A gentle spirit, that lightly did delay
Hot *Titans* beames, which then did glyster fayre:
When I whom sullein care,
Through discontent of my long fruitlesse stay
In Princes Court, and expectation vayne
Of idle hopes, which still doe fly away,
Like empty shaddowes, did aflict my brayne,
Walkt forth to ease my payne
Along the shoare of silver streaming *Themmes*,
Whose rutty Bancke, the which his River hemmes,
Was paynted all with variable flowers,
And all the meades adornd with daintie gemmes,
Fit to decke maydens bowres,
And crowne their Paramours,
Against the Brydale day, which is not long:
    Sweete *Themmes* runne softly, till I end my Song.

2

There, in a Meadow, by the Rivers side,
A Flocke of *Nymphes* I chaunced to espy,
All lovely Daughters of the Flood thereby,
With goodly greenish locks all loose untyde,
As each had bene a Bryde,
And each one had a little wicker basket,
Made of fine twigs entrayled curiously,

In which they gathered flowers to fill their flasket:
And with fine Fingers, cropt full feateously
The tender stalkes on hye.
Of every sort, which in that Meadow grew,
They gathered some; the Violet pallid blew,
The little Dazie, that at evening closes,
The virgin Lillie, and the Primrose trew,
With store of vermeil Roses,
To decke their Bridegromes posies,
Against the Brydale day, which was not long:
   Sweete *Themmes* runne softly, till I end my Song.

3

With that I saw two Swannes of goodly hewe,
Come softly swimming downe along the Lee;
Two fairer Birds I yet did never see:
The snow which doth the top of *Pindus* strew,
Did never whiter shew,
Nor *Jove* himselfe when he a Swan would be
For love of *Leda*, whiter did appeare:
Yet *Leda* was they say as white as he,
Yet not so white as these, nor nothing neare;
So purely white they were,
That even the gentle streame, the which them bare,
Seem'd foule to them, and bad his billowes spare
To wet their silken feathers, least they might
Soyle their fayre plumes with water not so fayre,
And marre their beauties bright,
That shone as heavens light,
Against their Brydale day, which was not long:
   Sweete *Themmes* runne softly, till I end my Song.

4

Eftsoones the *Nymphes*, which now had Flowers their fill,
Ran all in haste, to see that silver brood,
As they came floating on the Christal Flood,
Whom when they sawe, they stood amazed still,
Their wondring eyes to fill.
Them seem'd they never saw a sight so fayre,
Of Fowles so lovely, that they sure did deeme
Them heavenly borne, or to be that same payre
Which through the Skie draw *Venus* silver Teeme,
For sure they did not seeme
To be begot of any earthly Seede,
But rather Angels or of Angels breede:
Yet were they bred of *Somers-heat* they say,
In sweetest Season, when each Flower and weede
The earth did fresh aray,
So fresh they seem'd as day,
Even as their Brydale day, which was not long:
  Sweete *Themmes* runne softly, till I end my Song.

5

Then forth they all out of their baskets drew
Great store of Flowers, the honour of the field,
That to the sense did fragrant odours yield,
All which upon those goodly Birds they threw,
And all the Waves did strew,
That like old *Peneus* Waters they did seeme,
When downe along by pleasant *Tempes* shore
Scattred with Flowres, through *Thessaly* they streeme,
That they appeare through Lillies plenteous store,
Like a Brydes Chamber flore:
Two of those *Nymphes*, meane while, two Garlands bound,

Of freshest Flowres which in that Mead they found,
The which presenting all in trim Array,
Their snowie Foreheads therewithall they crownd,
Whil'st one did sing this Lay,
Prepar'd against that Day,
Against their Brydale day, which was not long:
   Sweete *Themmes* runne softly, till I end my Song.

6

Ye gentle Birdes, the worlds faire ornament,
And heavens glorie, whom this happie hower
Doth leade unto your lovers blisfull bower,
Joy may you have and gentle hearts content
Of your loves couplement:
And let faire *Venus*, that is Queene of love,
With her heart-quelling Sonne upon you smile,
Whose smile they say, hath vertue to remove
All Loves dislike, and friendships faultie guile
For ever to assoile.
Let endlesse Peace your steadfast hearts accord,
And blessed Plentie wait upon your bord,
And let your bed with pleasures chast abound,
That fruitfull issue may to you afford,
Which may your foes confound,
And make your joyes redound,
Upon your Brydale day, which is not long:
   Sweete *Themmes* run softlie, till I end my Song.

7

So ended she; and all the rest around
To her redoubled that her undersong,
Which said, their bridale daye should not be long.

And gentle Eccho from the neighbour ground,
Their accents did resound.
So forth those joyous Birdes did passe along,
Adowne the Lee, that to them murmurde low,
As he would speake, but that he lackt a tong,
Yet did by signes his glad affection show,
Making his streame run slow.
And all the foule which in his flood did dwell
Gan flock about these twaine, that did excell
The rest, so far, as *Cynthia* doth shend
The lesser starres. So they enranged well,
Did on those two attend,
And their best service lend,
Against their wedding day, which was not long:
    Sweete *Themmes* run softly, till I end my song.

8

At length they all to mery *London* came,
To mery London, my most kyndly Nurse,
That to me gave this Lifes first native sourse:
Though from another place I take my name,
An house of auncient fame.
There when they came, whereas those bricky towres,
The which on *Themmes* brode aged backe doe ryde,
Where now the studious Lawyers have their bowers,
There whylome wont the Templer Knights to byde,
Till they decayd through pride:
Next whereunto there standes a stately place,
Where oft I gayned giftes and goodly grace
Of that great Lord, which therein wont to dwell,
Whose want too well, now feeles my freendles case:
But Ah here fits not well

Olde woes but joyes to tell
Against the bridale daye, which is not long:
   Sweete *Themmes* runne softly, till I end my Song.

9

Yet therein now doth lodge a noble Peer,
Great *Englands* glory and the Worlds wide wonder,
Whose dreadfull name, late through all *Spaine* did thunder,
And *Hercules* two pillors standing neere,
Did make to quake and feare:
Faire branch of Honor, flower of Chevalrie,
That fillest *England* with thy triumphes fame,
Joy have thou of thy noble victorie,
And endlesse happinesse of thine owne name
That promiseth the same:
That through thy prowesse and victorious armes,
Thy country may be freed from forraine harmes:
And great *Elisaes* glorious name may ring
Through al the world, fil'd with thy wide Alarmes,
Which some brave muse may sing
To ages following,
Upon the Brydale day, which is not long:
   Sweete *Themmes* runne softly, till I end my Song.

10

From those high Towers, this noble Lord issuing,
Like Radiant *Hesper* when his golden hayre
In th'*Ocean* billowes he hath Bathed fayre,
Descended to the Rivers open vewing,
With a great traine ensuing.
Above the rest were goodly to bee seene
Two gentle Knights of lovely face and feature

Beseeming well the bower of anie Queene,
With gifts of wit and ornaments of nature,
Fit for so goodly stature:
That like the twins of *Jove* they seem'd in sight,
Which decke the Bauldricke of the Heavens bright.
They two forth pacing to the Rivers side,
Received those two faire Brides, their Loves delight,
Which at th'appointed tyde,
Each one did make his Bryde,
Against their Brydale day, which is not long:
   Sweete *Themmes* runne softly, till I end my Song.

from Notes for an Atlas

flowers of stone. A clatter of metal. And hear
the wash-away of water slapped from a shore.
And hear laughter and words in a language you
do not know. Read All the World's. See a man
with a glass and a jug of water. Sharp perfume
containing tea tree oil behind a cigarette smoke
veil. Read STORM CLIPPER. Slap of foamy
water, wash of curdled hissings and the crack of
water butchered by the shore. Rustle of plastic
and a whine of wind by increments up to a
sound which collapses to a buffeting noise in
the craters of the ears. See a row of faces in a
dark building like monkeys of silence. Hear the
grinding screel of a train's wheels. Hear,
'Upstairs, on.' Hear, 'Can we go on the?'
Wind running downriver like a shoal of flying
cars cutting up the water, up into flying and
curl-fallen peelings from a grater and the river's
underwater like a bituminous treacle creeps. A
man crying. Bridge-strings played by the wind,
aeolian harp of a suspension cable. Hear, 'I
suspect the design of this is quite formidable,
so there's just.' Hear a sound like a fanbelt of
traffic continuously and the wind makes a
moan. Trains and a bridge of two towers like a
forked tongue. See steam rising into an
elephant's head of steam from a trunk of steam
and its body breaks up into darkness. Water
strummed by wind to a frown of ripples hitting
a stone and the wind skates like a foot on a

skate and the wind straddles each shore of the
river with lapping splashes and sound ploughed
out of motion like an excess. Dark grey of a flat
stone. See buildings like strewn cut rocks in a
quarry. Square chimney and air fluttery at your
head, turn left at the neck to see water's shivery
fever of streams crossing stream, wind-streaked
serrations of panicky river, flat, black, smooth
surface like oil and you pass. Hear a metronome
of a walk. Two policemen together and see one
helmeted face looking down onto pavement
and one helmeted face with its eyes caught in
the sky. Read CITY OF LONDON. Pale
potato chips on paving. Hear voices grow and
hear voices fade. Read OXO. Letters of red
light. Squeak of brakes twice. Read 020 7248
2916. Flutter of a palm's fronds like black,
flexible knives lashing about. A single red light
like a live volcano seen from the air. Silverish
trees on the far shore. A ring's shine like a
crescent moon on the finger of a man. A coiled
fish of iron. Hear traffic prowling. Read toilet.
See an iron fish twisted in the body and coiled
around the foot of a lamp post. Man in dark
clothes rising from a wooden bench to walk and
he walks with feet not leaving the ground. Hear
noises of traffic and see two arches of a bridge
and read SEA CONTAINERS HOUSE. Hear
voices gathered together. See roses apart and
shiny leaves below flesh-pink flowers, the leaves
like small black canoes stranded within the
tree. See a mouth grinning, and pass, and hear
traffic make its crossings each way across the

flowing water and screels of the metal wheels of a train moving also. See iron columns rising from water like legs. A sphere of light. Damp spots on a step. A girl islanded in traffic. See scaffolding poles. See a chain of lights strung and the wind moves the whole chain slightly to bow inland from the river's stream. See black-branched trees and you look up to stone figures lit by lights and one shadow like an obelisk is cast up over the stone cheek of a face. See a girl with black eyes carrying full bags and see a stone horse climbing out from one wall of a building. A hall of words written on stone. An iron grate and the wind beats. See lights in windows and a room dull by lightbulb. A jogging man pauses. See three people ahead and look to the scrawl of trees black against sky. Hear, 'I'm still okay.' Voice of a girl in a red top. Black hull of a metal boat, there are rivets visible and you see rust leaked from paint. Man with a single dreadlock pushed into his lefthand trouser pocket. READ HMS PRESIDENT. Look to the lit portholes of a passing plane. See benches with cast iron legs like the legs of camels and see golden parts to the arms of each bench. See two slices of lemon lying shrunken under one bench. Read DELAYS POSSIBLE. See opening buds of a tree and a dark space of shrubs and grasses. Hexagons of concrete. Read POLICE. See lit windows uninhabited. An old

The Man-Moth*

       Here, above,
cracks in the buildings are filled with battered moonlight.
The whole shadow of Man is only as big as his hat.
It lies at his feet like a circle for a doll to stand on,
and he makes an inverted pin, the point magnetized to the moon.
He does not see the moon; he observes only her vast properties,
feeling the queer light on his hands, neither warm nor cold,
of a temperature impossible to record in thermometers.

       But when the Man-Moth
pays his rare, although occasional, visits to the surface,
the moon looks rather different to him. He emerges
from an opening under the edge of one of the sidewalks
and nervously begins to scale the faces of the buildings.
He thinks the moon is a small hole at the top of the sky,
proving the sky quite useless for protection.
He trembles, but must investigate as high as he can climb.

       Up the façades,
his shadow dragging like a photographer's cloth behind him,
he climbs fearfully, thinking that this time he will manage
to push his small head through that round clean opening
and be forced through, as from a tube, in black scrolls on the
    light.
(Man, standing below him, has no such illusions.)
But what the Man-Moth fears most he must do, although
he fails, of course, and falls back scared but quite unhurt.

       Then he returns
to the pale subways of cement he calls his home. He flits,
he flutters, and cannot get aboard the silent trains

fast enough to suit him. The doors close swiftly.
The Man-Moth always seats himself facing the wrong way
and the train starts at once at its full, terrible speed,
without a shift in gears or a gradation of any sort.
He cannot tell the rate at which he travels backwards.

      Each night he must
be carried through artificial tunnels and dream recurrent dreams.
Just as the ties recur beneath his train, these underlie
his rushing brain. He does not dare look out the window,
for the third rail, the unbroken draught of poison,
runs there beside him. He regards it as a disease
he has inherited the susceptibility to. He has to keep
his hands in his pockets, as others must wear mufflers.

      If you catch him,
hold up a flashlight to his eye. It's all dark pupil,
an entire night itself, whose haired horizon tightens
as he stares back, and closes up the eye. Then from the lids
one tear, his only possession, like the bee's sting, slips.
Slyly he palms it, and if you're not paying attention
he'll swallow it. However, if you watch, he'll hand it over,
cool as from underground springs and pure enough to drink.

* Newspaper misprint for 'mammoth'.

Song Cycle of the Moon-Bone

I

The people are making a camp of branches in that country at
    Arnhem Bay:
With the forked stick, the rail for the whole camp, the Mandjikai
    people are making it.
Branches and leaves are about the mouth of the hut: the middle is
    clear within.
They are thinking of rain, and of storing their clubs in case of a
    quarrel,
In the country of the Dugong, towards the wide clay-pans made
    by the Moonlight.
Thinking of rain, and of storing the fighting sticks.
They put up the rafters of arm-band-tree wood, put the branches
    on to the camp, at Arnhem Bay, in that place of the Dugong . . .
And they block up the back of the hut with branches.
Carefully place the branches, for this is the camp of the Morning-
    Pigeon man,
And of the Middle-of-the-Camp man; of the Mangrove-Fish man;
    of two other head-men,
And of the Clay-pan man; of the Baijini-Anchor man, and of the
    Arnhem Bay country man;
Of the Whale man and of another head-man: of the Arnhem Bay
    Creek man;
Of the Scales-of-the-Rock-Cod man; of the Rock Cod man, and
    of the Place-of-the-Water man.

II

They are sitting about in the camp, among the branches, along the
    back of the camp:

Sitting along in lines in the camp, there in the shade of the
     paperbark trees:
Sitting along in a line, like the new white spreading clouds;
In the shade of the paperbarks, they are sitting resting like clouds.
People of the clouds, living there like the mist; like the mist sitting
     resting with arms on knees,
In here towards the shade, in this Place, in the shadow of
     paperbarks
Sitting there in rows, those Wonguri-Mandjikai people, paperbark
     along like a cloud.
Living on cycad-nut bread; sitting there with white-stained
     fingers,
Sitting in there resting, those people of the Sandfly clan . . .
Sitting there like mist, at that place of the Dugong . . . and of the
     Dugong's Entrails . . .
Sitting resting there in the place of the Dugong . . .
In that place of the Moonlight Clay Pans, and at the place of the
     Dugong . . .
There at that Dugong place they are sitting all along.

III

Wake up from sleeping! Come, we go to see the clay pan, at the
     place of the Dugong . . .
Walking along, stepping along, straightening up after resting:
Walking along, looking as we go down on to the clay pan.
Looking for lily plants as we go . . . and looking for lily foliage . . .
Circling around, searching towards the middle of the lily leaves to
     reach the rounded roots.
At that place of the Dugong . . .
At that place of the Dugong's Tail . . .
At that place of the Dugong; looking for food with stalks,
For lily foliage, and for the round-nut roots of the lily plant.

IV

The birds saw the people walking along.
Crying, the white cockatoos flew over the clay pan of the
    Moonlight;
From the place of the Dugong they flew, looking for lily-root
    food; pushing the foliage down and eating the soft roots.
Crying, the birds flew down and along the clay pan, at that place
    of the Dugong . . .
Crying, flying down there along the clay pan . . .
At the place of the Dugong, of the Tree-Limbs-Rubbing-Together,
    and of the Evening Star.
Where the lily-root clay pan is . . .
Where the cockatoos play, at that place of the Dugong . . .
Flapping their wings they flew down, crying, 'We saw the people!'
There they are always living, those clans of the white cockatoo . . .
And there is the Shag woman, and there her clan:
Birds, trampling the lily foliage, eating the soft round roots!

V

An animal track is running along: it is the track of the rat . . .
Of the male rat, and the female rat, and the young that hang to
    her teats as she runs,
The male rat hopping along, and the female rat, leaving
    paw-marks as a sign . . .
On the clay pans of the Dugong, and in the shade of the trees,
At the Dugong's place, and at the place of her Tail . . .
Thus, they spread paw-mark messages all along their tracks,
In that place of the Evening Star, in the place of the Dugong . . .
Among the lily plants and into the mist, into the Dugong place,
    and into the place of her Entrails.
Backwards and forwards the rats run, always hopping along . . .

Carrying swamp-grass for nesting, over the little tracks, leaving
their signs.
Backwards and forwards they run on the clay pan, around the
place of the Dugong.
Men saw their tracks at the Dugong's place, in the shade of the
trees, on the white clay;
Roads of the rats, paw-marks everywhere, running into the mist.
All around are their signs; and there men saw them down on the
clay pan, at the place of the Dugong.

VI

A duck comes swooping down to the Moonlight clay pan, there at
the place of the Dugong . . .
From far away. 'I saw her flying over, in here at the clay pan . . .'
Floating along, pushing the pool into ripples and preening her
feathers.
'I carried these eggs from a long way off, from inland to Arnhem
Bay . . .'
Eggs, eggs, eggs; eggs she is carrying, swimming along.
She preens her feathers, and pulls at the lily foliage,
Drags at the lily leaves with her claws for food.
Swimming along, rippling the water among the lotus plants . . .
Backwards and forwards: she pulls at the foliage, swimming along,
floating and eating.
This bird is taking her food, the lotus food in the clay pan,
At the place of the Dugong there, at the place of the Dugong's
Tail . . .
Swimming along for food, floating, and rippling the water, there
at the place of the Lilies.
Taking the lotus, the rounded roots and stalks of the lily;
searching and eating there as she ripples the water.
'Because I have eggs, I give to my young the sound of the water.'

Splashing and preening herself, she ripples the water, among the
    lotus . . .
Backwards and forwards, swimming along, rippling the water,
Floating along on the clay pan, at the place of the Dugong.

VII

People were diving here at the place of the Dugong . . .
Here they were digging all around, following up the lily stalks,
Digging into the mud for the rounded roots of the lily,
Digging them out at that place of the Dugong, and of the Evening
    Star,
Pushing aside the water while digging, and smearing themselves
    with mud . . .
Piling up the mud as they dug, and washing the roots clean.
They saw arm after arm there digging: people thick like the
    mist . . .
The Shag woman too was there, following up the lily stalks.
There they saw arm after arm of the Mandjikai Sandfly clan,
Following the stalks along, searching and digging for food:
Always there together, those Mandjikai Sandfly people.
They follow the stalks of the lotus and lily, looking for food.
The lilies that always grow there at the place of the Dugong . . .
At that clay pan, at the place of the Dugong, at the place of the lilies.

VIII

Now the leech is swimming along . . . It always lives there in the
    water . . .
It takes hold of the leaves of the lily and pods of the lotus, and
    climbs up on to their stalks.
Swimming along and grasping hold of the leaves with its head . . .
It always lives there in the water, and climbs up on to the people.
Always there, that leech, together with all its clan . . .

Swimming along towards the trees, it climbs up and waits for
    people.
Hear it swimming along through the water, its head out ready to
    grasp us . . .
Always living here and swimming along.
Because that leech is always there, for us, however it came there:
The leech that catches hold of those Mandjikai Sandfly people . . .

IX

The prawn is there, at the place of the Dugong, digging out mud
    with its claws . . .
The hard-shelled prawn living there in the water, making soft little
    noises.
It burrows into the mud and casts it aside, among the lilies . . .
Throwing aside the mud, with soft little noises . . .
Digging out mud with its claws at the place of the Dugong, the
    place of the Dugong's Tail . . .
Calling the bone bukalili, the catfish bukalili, the frog bukalili, the
    sacred tree bukalili . . .
The prawn is burrowing, coming up, throwing aside the mud, and
    digging . . .
Climbing up on to the lotus plants and on to their pods . . .

X

Swimming along under the water, as bubbles rise to the surface,
    the tortoise moves in the swamp grass.
Swimming among the lily leaves and the grasses, catching them as
    she moves . . .
Pushing them with her short arms. Her shell is marked with designs,
This tortoise carrying her young, in the clay pan, at the place of
    the Dugong . . .
The short-armed Mararlpa tortoise, with special arm-bands, here
    at the place of the Dugong . . .

Backwards and forwards she swims, the short-armed one of the
    Mararlpa, and the Dalwongu.
Carrying eggs about, in the clay pan, at the place of the Dugong . . .
Her entrails twisting with eggs . . .
Swimming along through the grass, and moving her patterned shell.
The tortoise with her young, and her special arm-bands,
Swimming along, moving her shell, with bubbles rising;
Throwing out her arms towards the place of the Dugong . . .
This creature with the short arms, swimming and moving her shell;
This tortoise, swimming along with the drift of the water . . .
Swimming with her short arms, at the place of the Dugong . . .

XI

Wild-grape vines are floating there in the billabong:
Their branches, joint by joint, spreading over the water.
Their branches move as they lie, backwards and forwards,
In the wind and the waves, at the Moonlight clay pan, at the place
    of the Dugong . . .
Men see them lying there on the clay pan pool, in the shade of the
    paperbarks:
Their spreading limbs shift with the wind and the water:
Grape vines with their berries . . .
Blown backwards and forwards as they lie, there at the place of
    the Dugong.
Always there, with their hanging grapes, in the clay pan of the
    Moonlight . . .
Vine plants and roots and jointed limbs, with berry food,
    spreading over the water.

XII

Now the New Moon is hanging, having cast away his bone:
Gradually he grows larger, taking on new bone and flesh.

Over there, far away, he has shed his bone: he shines on the place
    of the Lotus Root, and the place of the Dugong,
On the place of the Evening Star, of the Dugong's Tail, of the
    Moonlight clay pan . . .
His old bone gone, now the New Moon grows larger;
Gradually growing, his new bone growing as well.
Over there, the horns of the old receding Moon bent down, sank
    into the place of the Dugong:
His horns were pointing towards the place of the Dugong.
Now the New Moon swells to fullness, his bone grown larger.
He looks on the water, hanging above it, at the place of the Lotus.
There he comes into sight, hanging above the sea, growing larger
    and older . . .
There far away he has come back, hanging over the clans near
    Milingimbi . . .
Hanging there in the sky, above those clans . . .
'Now I'm becoming a big moon, slowly regaining my
    roundness' . . .
In the far distance the horns of the Moon bend down, above
    Milingimbi,
Hanging a long way off, above Milingimbi Creek . . .
Slowly the Moon Bone is growing, hanging there far away.
The bone is shining, the horns of the Moon bend down.
First the sickle Moon on the old Moon's shadow; slowly he grows.
And shining he hangs there at the place of the Evening Star . . .
Then far away he goes sinking down, to lose his bone in the sea;
Diving towards the water, he sinks down out of sight.
The old Moon dies to grow new again, to rise up out of the sea.

XIII

Up and up soars the Evening Star, hanging there in the sky.
Men watch it, at the place of the Dugong and of the Clouds, and
    of the Evening Star.

A long way off, at the place of Mist, of Lilies and of the Dugong.
The Lotus, the Evening Star, hangs there on its long stalk, held by
    the Spirits.
It shines on that place of the Shade, on the Dugong place, and on
    to the Moonlight clay pan . . .
The Evening Star is shining, back towards Milingimbi, and over
    the Wulamba people . . .
Hanging there in the distance, towards the place of the Dugong,
The place of the Eggs, of the Tree-Limbs-Rubbing-Together, and
    of the Moonlight clay pan . . .
Shining on its short stalk, the Evening Star, always there at the clay
    pan, at the place of the Dugong . . .
There, far away, the long string hangs at the place of the Evening
    Star, the place of the Lilies.
Away there at Milingimbi . . . at the place of the Full Moon,
Hanging above the head of that Wonguri tribesman:
The Evening Star goes down across the camp, among the white
    gum trees . . .
Far away, in those places near Milingimbi . . .
Goes down among the Ngurulwulu people, towards the camp and
    the gum trees,
At the place of the Crocodiles, and of the Evening Star, away
    towards Milingimbi . . .
The Evening Star is going down, the Lotus Flower on its stalk . . .
Going down among all those western clans . . .
It brushes the heads of the uncircumcised people . . .
Sinking down in the sky, that Evening Star, the Lotus . . .
Shining on to the foreheads of all those head-men . . .
On to the heads of all those Sandfly people . . .
It sinks there into the place of the white gum trees, at Milingimbi.

Translated by R. M. Berndt

from Briggflatts

Furthest, fairest things, stars, free of our humbug,
each his own, the longer known the more alone,
wrapt in emphatic fire roaring out to a black flue.
Each spark trills on a tone beyond chronological compass,
yet in a sextant's bubble present and firm
places a surveyor's stone or steadies a tiller.

BASIL BUNTING   [210

from Leaves of Grass: 31

I believe a leaf of grass is no less than the journeywork of the stars,
And the pismire is equally perfect, and a grain of sand, and the
    egg of the wren,
And the tree-toad is a chef-d'œuvre for the highest,
And the running blackberry would adorn the parlors of heaven,
And the narrowest hinge in my hand puts to scorn all machinery,
And the cow crunching with depressed head surpasses any statue,
And a mouse is miracle enough to stagger sextillions of infidels,
And I could come every afternoon of my life to look at the
    farmer's girl boiling her iron tea-kettle and baking shortcake.

I find I incorporate gneiss and coal and long-threaded moss and
    fruits and grains and esculent roots,
And am stucco'd with quadrupeds and birds all over,
And have distanced what is behind me for good reasons,
And call any thing close again when I desire it.

In vain the speeding or shyness,
In vain the plutonic rocks send their old heat against my approach,
In vain the mastodon retreats beneath its own powdered bones,
In vain objects stand leagues off and assume manifold shapes,
In vain the ocean settling in hollows and the great monsters lying
    low,
In vain the buzzard houses herself with the sky,
In vain the snake slides through the creepers and logs,
In vain the elk takes to the inner passes of the woods,
In vain the razorbilled auk sails far north to Labrador,
I follow quickly . . . I ascend to the nest in the fissure of the cliff.

WALT WHITMAN

Acknowledgements

ANON: 'Folklore' 1–4, translated by Tim Atkins from *Heart Hammer*
(Laird Hunt, Paris, 1995), reprinted with kind permission of the
translator. 'Song Cycle of the Moon Bone' translated by R. M. Bendt from
The Unwritten Song (Jonathan Cape, 1969). DANNIE ABSE: 'Song of a
Hebrew' from *The Penguin Book of Oral Poetry (Penguin*, 1982).
W. H AUDEN: 'In Praise of Limestone' from *Collected Poems* (Faber, 1976).
JOHN ASHBERY: 'Into the Dusk-Charged Air' from *Selected Poems*
(Penguin Press, 1994), by permission of Carcanet Press. SAMUEL
BECKETT: from 'An Abandoned Work' from *Six Residua* (John Calder,
1989). WENDELL BERRY: 'How long does it take to make the woods' from
Sabbath (North Point Press, 1987). ELIZABETH BISHOP: 'The Man-Moth'
from *Complete Poems* (Chatto & Windus, 1991). SEAN BORODALE: 'Notes
for an Atlas' reprinted by kind permission of the author. BASIL BUNTING:
'Briggflatts' from *Complete Poems*, edited by Richard Caddel (Bloodaxe
Books, 2000). JOHN BURNSIDE: 'Heat Wave' from *The Light Trap*
(Jonathan Cape), used by permission of the Random House Group
Limited. CHARLES CAUSLEY: 'Riley' and 'Tam Snow' from *Collected Poems*
(Macmillan, 1975), reprinted by permission of David Higham Associates.
AIME CESAIRE: 'Rains' from *Poetry of Surrealism* (Little Brown & Co. Inc.,
1974). HART CRANE: 'The Hurricane' from *Complete Poems* (Bloodaxe
Books, 1984). E. E. CUMMINGS: 'Spring is like a perhaps hand' from
Complete Poems 1904–1962, edited by George J. Firmage, by permission of
W. W. Norton & Company. Copyright © 1991 by the Trustees for the
E. E. Cummings Trust and George James Firmage. W. H. DAVIES:
'Cowslips and Larks' from Complete Poems (Jonathan Cape, 1963),
reprinted by permission of the Will Trust of Mrs. H. M. Davies. IAN
HAMILTON FINLAY: 'Estuary' and 'The Ascent of the Lark' published by
Wild Hawthorn Press, Little Sparta, Dunsyre, Scotland. Reprinted by kind
permission of the author. ROBERT FROST: 'Putting in the Seed' and
'Mowing' from *The Poetry of Robert Frost*, edited by Edward Connery
Lathem (Jonathan Cape), published by permission of the Estate of Robert
Frost and The Random House Group Limited. ALAN GINSBERG: 'In
back of the real' from *Howl and Other Poems* (City Lights, 1959).

WOODY GUTHRIE: 'Pastures of Plenty' from *The Penguin Book of Oral Poetry* (Penguin, 1982). DAVID HART: 'Naming the Field' from *Field Days* (Green Books, 1998), reprinted by kind permission of the author. SEAMUS HEANEY: 'Bog Queen' from *North* (Faber and Faber, 1975); '[The Trees of Ireland]' from *Sweeney Astray* (Faber and Faber, 1992). TED HUGHES: 'Wodwo' from *Wodwo* (Faber and Faber, 1967); 'Snow and Snow' from *Season Songs* (Faber and Faber, 1976); 'Glimpse' from *Crow* (Faber and Faber, 1970); 'In the Likeness of a Grasshopper' from *Flowers and Insects*, 1986. DAVID JONES: from I*n Parenthesis* (Faber and Faber, 1937). JAMES JOYCE: 'Chamber Music XXXV' from *James Joyce: Selected Poems and Shorter Prose* (Faber and Faber). PATRICK KAVANAGH: 'Canal Bank Walk' from *Selected Poems* (Penguin, 1996). RUDYARD KIPLING: 'The Last Chantey' from *Kipling's Verse* (Hodder and Stoughton). NORMAN MCCAIG: 'A Voice of Summer' from *Collected Poems* (Chatto & Windus). HUGH MACDIARMID: 'The Wreck of the *Swan*' from *Complete Poems* (Carcanet, 1993). MACK MAZE: 'If You See my Mother' from *The Penguin Book of Oral Poetry* (Penguin, 1982). DUNAN BAN MACINTYRE: 'The Praise of Ben Dorain', translated by Hugh Macdiarmid, from *Complete Poems* (Carcanet, 1993). F. T. MARINETTI: 'A Landscape Heard' from *Poems for the Millennium* (University of California Press, 1995). JOHN MASEFIELD: from 'Reynard the Fox' reprinted by permission of the Society of Authors as the Literary Representative of the Estate of John Masefield. MARIANNE MOORE: 'The Frigate Pelican' from *Collected Poems* (Faber and Faber, 1956). LES MURRAY: 'The Emerald Dove' and 'Thinking about Aboriginal Land Rights' from *Collected Poems* (Carcanet, 1998). VITEZSLAW NEZVAL: 'Trap Door' from *Poems for the Millennium* (University of California Press, 1995). JACQUES PREVERT: 'To Paint the Portrait of a Bird' from *Poetry of Surrealism* (Little Brown & Co, Inc., 1974). FRANCES PONGE: 'Moss', translated by C. K. Williams from *Selected Poems* (Faber and Faber). KATRINA PORTEOUS: 'The Wund an' the Wetter' from The Wund an' the Wetter (Iron Press, 1999). VASKO POPA: 'The Seed' from Vasko Popa: Collected Poems, translated by Anne Pennington, revised and expanded by Francis R. Jones (Anvil Press, 1997). THEODORE ROETHKE: 'Ballad of the Clairvoyant Widow' from *Collected Poems* (Faber and Faber, 1966). STEVIE SMITH: 'I may be smelly and I may be old' from *Collected Poems* (Penguin Books, 1975). GARY SNYDER: 'Boat of a Million Years', from *Mountains and Rivers without End* (Counterpoint Press, 1997). DYLAN THOMAS: 'Over St John's Hill' from *Collected Poems* (Dent), reprinted by permission of David Higham

Associates. RUSKIN WATTS: from 'Easter Rex' from Odes and Episodes (2002), reprinted with kind permission of the author. SANDOR WEORES: 'The Lost Parasol', translated by Edwin Morgan, from *Eternal Moment* (Anvil Press, 1988).

Index of Poets